SATAN
IS
REAL

REAL

THE BALLAD OF THE **LOUVIN BROTHERS**

CHARLIE LOUVIN
WITH **BENJAMIN WHITMER**

itbooks
AN IMPRINT OF HARPERCOLLINS PUBLISHER

IGNITER
LITERARY
GROUP

HarperCollins books may be purchased for educational, business, or sales promotional use. For information please write: Special Markets Department, HarperCollins Publishers, 10 East 53rd Street, New York, NY 10022.

FIRST EDITION

Designed by Meat & Potatoes, Inc.

Library of Congress Cataloging-in-Publication Data is available upon request.

ISBN: 978-0-06-206903-0

12 13 14 15 16 DIX/QG 10 9 8 7 6 5 4 3 2

Lyrics Permissions. **Knoxville Girl** © 1959 Sony/ATV Music Publishing LLC. All rights administered by Sony/ATV Music Publishing LLC, 8 Music Square West, Nashville, TN 37203. All rights reserved. Used by permission • **The Kneeling Drunkard's Plea** © 1949 Sony/ATV Music Publishing LLC. All rights administered by Sony/ATV Music Publishing LLC, 8 Music Square West, Nashville, TN 37203. All rights reserved. Used by permission • **Great Atomic Power** © 1952 Sony/ATV Music Publishing LLC. All rights administered by Sony/ATV Music Publishing LLC, 8 Music Square West, Nashville, TN 37203. All rights reserved. Used by permission • **Ira** Courtesy of Tompkins Square Music Publishing (Administered by Spirit One Music) (BMI)

Photo credits appear on page 301.

For my sons Sonny, Glenn, and Kenneth. There's an old song by Moe Bandy called "Till I'm Too Old to Die Young." The words go, "Let me watch my children grow to see what they've become. Oh Lord, don't let that cold wind blow till I'm too old to die young." Life has been good to me, and I don't have to worry about that song no more. I've been blessed in that I've seen you grow up to be great men, all of you.

And for my wife, Betty. I remember when the country singer Carl Smith's wife died, and I went to her funeral. Carl was the steadiest man I'd ever met, just as solid as a table. But when they were doing the last eulogy, he absolutely went to pieces. It shook me up so bad that I had to go out into the yard to get over it. And right there in the yard, I prayed to God for one request, that whenever I go, I'd go before you. I'm just not that tough that I could make it without you. I know that. Just as I know that I've needed you with me every step of the way.

Somebody's gonna hear my side before this thing is over,
Rough and rugged, burning careers in flames,
Somebody's gonna hear my side before this thing is over,
Playin' our songs, hopin' you'll remember our names.

—Alan Clinger and Roy Allen Pace, "Makin' Music"

CONTENTS

FOREWORD
BY KRIS KRISTOFFERSON

The legendary Louvin Brothers' hauntingly beautiful Appalachian blood harmony is truly one of the treasures of American music. I met Charlie and his wife, Betty, some years after the death of brother Ira when he was recording at the studio where I was working as a janitor. One nice thing about meeting a hero when you're a nobody is you learn how nice they really are. We've been friends ever since, meeting at jam sessions at Johnny Cash's house. The last time I saw him was backstage after a concert at the old Ryman Auditorium. As usual, we were always smiling as soon as we saw each other.

I'm grateful for the music and laughter we shared. This autobiography is as real and as moving as his music. My heart goes out to his wife, Betty, and his sons Sonny, Glenn, and Kenneth.

CHAPTER 1

MY
BROTHER'S
KEEPER

My older brother Ira and I were finishing a stretch of shows, the last in Georgia, and we decided to stop by Mama and Papa's place on Sand Mountain for a quick visit. Of course, we'd barely got on the road before Ira reached under his seat and pulled out a bottle of whiskey, and he drank the whole damn thing on the drive. When I pulled up to the house, I stepped out on my side, and Ira just kind of poured himself out on his.

Mama was out in the front yard, and you could tell how excited she was to see us. She came running up to try to hug Ira, but he put his arm out to hold her off. He was wobbling on his feet, barely able to stand upright.

She knew what was going on. Mamas know everything. "Aw, honey," she said, "Why do you have to do this to yourself?" She wouldn't even take Communion in a church unless they had grape juice instead of wine. She didn't use alcohol and she didn't understand anybody who did.

She should have known better than to say that, though. Nothing pissed Ira off like when somebody tried to put a little guilt on him. "Aw, leave me alone," he said. "I ain't hurting nobody."

"You're hurting yourself," she said. "That's who you're hurting."

"Yeah, well, I don't remember asking you," he said, and tried to light a cigarette. He was so drunk he couldn't even get his lighter to make a flame. "Goddamn it," he said.

"That whiskey don't do you no good," she said. "It don't do nobody no good."

Finally, he got his lighter to work, and he poked his mouth at the fire to light the cigarette, but he missed.

"Your father's in Knoxville," she continued. "I sure am glad he's not here right now to see you like this."

Ira threw the still unlit cigarette on the ground. "Will you shut up, bitch?"

I can guarantee you the fucking fight was on then. I beat the shit out of him right there in the front yard. He was lucky it was just words, too. If he'd have touched her, I'd still be in prison. Shit, if Papa was there, he might have killed him anyway, but I just kicked his ass all over the place. Then I stuffed him in the car, and we drove away.

"I know you ain't asleep," I said to him once we got on the highway. He was curled up on his side of the car, holding his busted face. "I'm only gonna tell you this once. If you talk to her like that again, I'll beat the shit out of you again. I'll do it every time. You can lump it or try to change it, but that's the way it is."

"Oh, hell, I didn't mean nothing by it," he slurred. "That was just that old whiskey talking."

"That ain't no excuse," I said. "Nobody forced you to drink that stuff. And you'd better not ever do it again."

Then I stopped talking and just drove, fuming. And

I thought about that day, nineteen years ago, when I saw Roy Acuff driving past the farm in his big air-cooled Franklin. I thought it must be just about the best thing on earth to ride in a car like that. Now I was driving down that same road, a Grand Ole Opry star in an automobile almost as nice, and it felt like I was suffocating. Like I was being buried alive in it.

CHAPTER 2

AN
AIR-COOLED
FRANKLIN

It was a warm afternoon in early autumn. The sky was clear blue and the sun was shining down, but it wasn't burning hot like it had been most of the summer. Papa was using the mules to pull a stalk chopper in one of the fields we'd picked clean, cutting the cotton stalks into the ground. You couldn't till for the next crop of cotton unless you got rid of those stalks, and chopping them into the soil returned some of what the cotton pulled out.

If there was any work at all Papa could find to do with the mules, he'd do it. He knew he had to keep them working if he wanted to make a living, just as he knew he had to keep his children working, too. He was a lean, hard, weather-beaten man, and even though he was only five foot, five inches tall, he had a way about him that made him look at least twice as big.

Even as hot as it was, he was wearing a long-sleeve shirt under his overalls, buttoned right up to the neck. I don't care if it was a hundred and five degrees in the shade, he wouldn't wear nothing else. Once that shirt got wet with sweat, he'd look at anybody who had peeled off their shirt in the heat and say in a satisfied voice, "Well, now I'm cooler than you are, ain't I?" That was one of his beliefs, that once you got wet with sweat, your shirt would help you catch the breeze.

My brother Ira and I were in another field picking the last of the season's cotton, pausing every few minutes to look over our shoulder for Roy Acuff's automobile to come tearing down the dirt road that ran by our farm. Ira was about sixteen and I was thirteen, and we'd been waiting for the singer and fiddler since we pulled on our cotton sacks and walked out of the house at sunrise to begin the day's work. There was nobody bigger than Roy Acuff to Ira and I.

We'd known that Roy Acuff would be driving past our house that day because Ed Watkins, who owned the mercantile store, had a radio in his living room. And the last Satur-

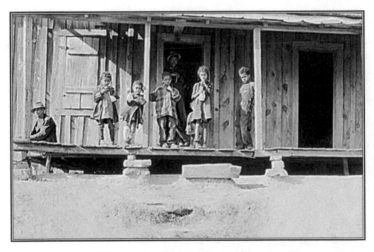

Sand Mountain, Alabama, sharecroppers in 1940

day, as soon as we got done in the cotton fields, Ira and I had run down to Watkins' house and joined all the other farmers on his porch to listen to the Grand Ole Opry. There was about twenty-five of us gathered in the dark of that porch, and then twenty-five more in the yellow light of Watkins' living room, leaning into his old radio.

Everybody knew what artists was going to be on at what time, and when their favorites came on, they stubbed out their cigarettes and moved inside to hear them, while the folks who were done listening to their favorites got up and came outside. Everybody on the porch was just as quiet as those inside. The radio was a little thing, not much of a speaker on it, and you had to really listen to hear what was going on. We did, and as soon as we heard Acuff being announced, it was our turn to go inside. We sat down on the rug, just as close to the radio as we could get.

Well, Acuff sang his songs, and we got up to leave. But just as we made it to our feet, we heard him start talking, announcing upcoming shows. When he got to the one next week at the Spring Hill School in Alabama, it felt like somebody had sucked all the air out of my lungs. Ira's eyes were as big as pie plates and I'll bet mine were the same. He grabbed me by the arm quick and pulled me outside, away from the porch so we could talk.

"Did you hear that, Charlie?" he asked in a whisper.

"That's our school," I blurted out.

"I know every road in this county. There's only one route he can take to get there, and it's right by our house."

"We're gonna see him drive by?"

"Yes, we are," Ira said. "And then we're gonna go see him play the show."

"How are we gonna do that, Ira? We ain't got no dime, neither one of us."

Well, Ira said he had a plan. And as we worked our way

down the rows of cotton that afternoon, I wondered what it was.

Of course, Mama and all our sisters were out there picking, too. Even though Mama did all the housework, she was always out there with us in the field when it came picking time. And, as usual, she had a little one with her, riding on her pick sack. Mama never cared for Roy Acuff much. She didn't really care for anybody on the radio. Most of the songs she liked were a hundred years old or more. And our sisters were completely uninterested in Acuff, too. He was known for being old-timey even then, and they liked the more modern music. So Ira and I paid them no attention at all.

Then Ira and I heard it. The roar of an automobile engine off in the distance, closing fast. We straightened up from pulling the cotton bolls, and there it come, ripping along not a hundred yards from our house, a trail of dust billowing out behind it, ROY ACUFF AND HIS SMOKY MOUNTAIN BOYS AND GIRLS painted all the way down the side. We'd never seen anything like that automobile. It had four doors on each side, and it was so long that I wondered that it didn't need hinges in the middle to navigate some of the turns in our crooked old road. We stood there holding our cotton sacks, watching it drive on until it disappeared in its own dust.

Then we bent over and got back to picking. We knew better than to let Papa catch us just standing around. "So how are we gonna get a dime to see that show?" I finally asked Ira as we filled our sacks.

"It's only a dime if you're trying to get inside," Ira said. "It won't cost us nothing to stand on the yard and listen. You know how hot that gymnasium gets. If they leave those windows closed, everybody in there'll suffocate to death. They'll have to open 'em, and then we'll be able to hear as good as anybody inside."

It was awful hard to argue with Ira when he had his mind

made up to convince you of something. And I didn't really need a whole lot of convincing, anyway. So we kept our eyes fixed on Papa, waiting for him to give us the go ahead to be done for the day, getting more scared every minute that we weren't going to make it to the show before it started.

Papa kept us working right up until sundown, too. I couldn't even tell you if we ate supper before we lit out for the show. We might've grabbed a hunk of corn bread on the way out the door. But I do know that we made the two miles to our school in ten minutes flat.

When we came to a stop in the schoolyard, we were glad to see that we weren't alone. The program hadn't started yet, but the high school gymnasium was packed with people, and there were more in the front yard than there was inside. At least three hundred of them, milling around, smoking cigarettes, making conversation, all of them straight out of the fields just like us. We were kindly thrilled to see them all. That way it wouldn't look as bad as if it was just us standing out there on the lawn by ourselves.

We mixed and mingled our way through the crowd, saying hello here and there. Moving closer and closer until we found the perfect spot, as close as we could get to the window and still be far enough back that we could stand on our tiptoes and see the show.

Suddenly, Roy Acuff appeared onstage. Behind him was a regular four-piece band, including a doghouse bass player, a guitar picker, Rachel Veach on banjo, and Bashful Brother Oswald with his dobro. Roy himself held a fiddle in his hand, but it was just his stage prop. He'd balance the bow on his nose from time to time, but you never did hear him play.

Rachel was wearing a nice gingham dress, but all the men was dressed in overalls and white shirts. The only one dressed a little different was Oswald, in his big floppy hat and over-sized shoes. I believe they thought overalls and white shirts

Sand Mountain farmers, 1937

represented country people, and I suppose they did. It was what we wore, anyway. I don't think I owned a pair of pants until I was grown and married. Rachel and Oswald also had some of their teeth blacked out with a pencil, which everybody thought was funny in those days, and in between songs, they'd clown around, pretending to be brother and sister.

Ira and I laughed at the funny parts, but mostly we was there to hear the songs. To judge them against the versions we'd heard on the Opry, and against the versions we sang for our friends and family. They played "Great Speckled Bird" and "Wabash Cannonball," both of which Ira and I knew by heart. And they played a gruesome old song about death that was older than anyone in Roy's band, probably from the seventeenth century. While the band was playing, we latched onto every note, every word. I could hear Ira breathing next to me, but I didn't dare turn away to look at him.

And then, just as quick as it started, it was over. By ten o'clock, they'd loaded their equipment into the car, waved at the crowd, and pulled off down the road. And watching them go, Ira and I had the same feeling. Like we was watching a funeral.

It was harvest time and the night was cool, but there was no big harvest moon as we walked home, just stars and clouds.

"Did you see the inside of that automobile?" I asked Ira.

"I saw it," he said. He was walking fast and fidgeting with his hands. I was probably as worked up as he was, but I was trying not to show it. "It was an air-cooled Franklin."

"How'd you figure that out?"

"I asked."

I was quiet for a few minutes. Walking for a few minutes, and then falling behind his long strides and having to run to catch up. "What do you think it's like to ride in a car like that?"

"It ain't like nothing we ever rode in," Ira said. "That's for sure."

"I ain't even ever seen one like it," I said. "How much do you think it cost him?"

"I can't even guess," Ira said.

"Well, then, how much money do you think he made tonight?"

"If he charged a quarter a person, I'd say he made more'n a hundred dollars."

"A hundred dollars," I said. "Buddy, that's money."

"It'd take Papa two months to earn that much," Ira said.

I hesitated. He almost seemed angry, so I wasn't sure I should say what I was thinking. But I said it anyway. "There was some of those songs I think we do as well as he does."

Ira didn't stop fidgeting with his hands, but he grinned. And I realized he hadn't been angry at all. He was just studying that same thought. "There are some we do even better," he said.

Because there were. We'd sung most of Acuff's songs. We knew them as well as he did, and the people on Sand Mountain liked our versions. Roy Acuff had triggered our love for country music. He was, of all things, true to his music. But, still, maybe we could do some of them a little better.

It took us nearly an hour to get home compared to the ten minutes it had taken coming the other way. Both of us lost in convincing ourselves that that's exactly what we're going to shoot for. That we were going to play on the Opry and tour in one of those air-cooled Franklins. We convinced ourselves until we just knew that we were going to do it.

The only trick left was how.

CHAPTER 3

PERSIMMONS

The problem with Ira, even at that age, was that he was never very patient. He didn't like to wait for his dreams to come true. He didn't like to wait to get anything he wanted.

For example, Papa had this persimmon tree down in the pasture. It was a pretty good-size one, maybe six inches in diameter, and Ira'd been watching it that summer for the persimmons to get ripe. It was loaded down with fruit, but the thing about persimmons is that if they ain't just about ready to fall off the tree when you pick 'em, they'll make you sicker'n a dog.

Well, one day Ira just couldn't take it anymore. He grabbed on to the tree and tried to shake it hard enough to knock some of them loose. And when that didn't work, he found himself a stick and beat the hell out of the trunk, hoping that would knock a few off, but they weren't nearly ripe enough to fall. So he walked around the tree for a while, looking it over and thinking. And then he told me, "Go get me the ax out of the house."

It didn't take a genius to figure out what that meant. "Papa ain't gonna like it if you chop down that tree just to get a persimmon," I said.

"You want a persimmon or don't you?" he said. "Get on up there to the house and get the ax."

I knew better, of course. Hell, I knew better the whole quarter mile up to the house. Papa counted on those persimmons for eating when they got ripe, and I knew exactly what would happen when he caught us. Which he would. There was no way we could chop down a tree and have it escape his notice. He knew every inch of his land.

Papa never whipped any of the girls, but neither of us boys were strangers to getting beaten. Especially Ira. If Papa was calm, just punishing us for doing something that we'd known was wrong, he'd find him a hickory limb about as big around as his thumb and whip us with it. He called it a width, and it'd wrap all the way around you. It'd hurt like hell, of course, and you'd scream and holler, but it wouldn't do any real damage.

Papa wasn't always calm when he came after Ira to give him a whipping, though. And when he wasn't calm, he wouldn't wait to find a width of hickory, he'd beat him with whatever was at hand. A chunk of firewood, a piece of furniture, whatever.

He didn't take into much account the reason for the whipping either. Or the state we were already in. One winter Ira and I'd been playing behind the wood stove in the kitchen. There was this little space back there where you could stack wood, and I had this hatchet I was fooling around with, swinging at chunks of wood. And Ira put his hand on the floor and said, "I'll bet you can't hit my hand with that thing."

I swung as quick as I could, but he scooted his hand back quicker. I was three years younger'n him, not more than seven, and I wasn't nearly as fast as he was. He laughed at me and scooted his hand toward me again to give me another try, and I swung again and missed again. He kept it up, scooting his hand out there and laughing at me, betting me I'd never be able to hit him.

Finally, I anticipated how long it'd take him to scoot his hand out there, and when he started moving, I started swinging at the same time, and I slammed that ax right down on his fingers. It was a sharp blade, and if I'd had any strength at all, he wouldn't have had any fingers left. As it was, he was bleeding everywhere. I'd cut him right down to the bone.

I got a whipping for that one, of course. "He wanted to play the game," I cried to Papa. But it didn't matter, he whipped me anyway. Not nearly as bad as he whipped Ira, though. He beat the shit out of him, and Ira with his fingers damn near cut off.

Even knowing that a whipping was a sure thing, Ira'd convinced me how bad I wanted a persimmon, even if they weren't quite ripe yet. So I walked all the way up to the house, and fetched the ax back. And when I gave it to Ira, he lit into that persimmon tree, chopping it about halfway through so we could pull it over and pick as many of those persimmons as we could reach.

After we'd got all the fruit off, we found us a pole a couple inches in diameter and about four or five feet long and used it to prop the tree back up. It was gonna die anyway, Ira'd chopped almost the whole way through, but he figured maybe we could hide what we'd done by propping it up with that pole. Then we turned to the persimmons, which were all too green to eat. We ate them anyways, all of 'em. We had to, to hide the evidence, if nothing else. And, of course, we got sicker'n hell.

Well, the next day, Papa was walking down in the pasture, and he saw that post in the ground next to the persimmon tree. And not knowing what it was, he kicked it out of the way. Of course, the whole fucking tree fell over on him.

He was furious. Almost possessed. He came roaring up into the house, all bleeding and banged up from the tree, and carrying the pole that Ira'd propped the tree up with. It was the most terrifying thing I'd ever seen.

Poor Ira tried to get away, running backward straight into a wall. "Charlie was there, too," he hollered, trying to put some of it off on me. "He's the one who got the ax."

But Papa didn't buy it. He got ahold of Ira and beat him with that post until Ira was just curled up on the floor protecting himself. And then he kept beating him until Ira couldn't move at all, until he was unconscious and bleeding. Mama finally got him to stop, holding on to his arm and begging until he threw the post down on the floor and stormed out the door.

"Ira," Mama said, holding his head and trying to wake him up. "Oh, Charlsey," she said to my sister. "Run and get the doctor. I can't get him to wake up."

Ira did finally come awake after the doctor came. And after a day or so of being taken care of by Mama, he was fine. Though I'm not sure he ever had a taste for persimmons again.

It worked out most of the time that way. Ira got the rough end of life as far as discipline, there's no doubt about it. He was the older one, and that meant Papa'd whip him not only for what it was that we'd done, but also for convincing me to go along with him. I knew what I was doing most of the time, but Ira got the beatings.

The problem was Papa had a rough life. He was born in Murphy, North Carolina. That's where all his people were from. His father was a drinker, and made his living selling charcoal. Back then, charcoal was a necessary for many folks, because it was what you'd use to get the old smoothing irons hot enough so you could iron with them. You could make a living selling it, but it was brutal work. And, of course, Papa's father didn't do most of the work himself. He made his kids do it.

They'd dig a hole, about six or seven foot square and maybe six foot deep. Then they'd chop up these pine timbers, lay them in the hole, and set them on fire. Once they got them burning good, they'd put enough dirt on top of them to smother them, and wait until they quit smoking under the dirt. And then the kids had to get down there and get the dirt off and shovel the charcoal out before it cooled.

It was so hot it'd melt the soles off their shoes and blister their feet. I can only imagine it. It must've seemed to Papa like he was being forced to work in Hell itself. And their father would be up on the edge of the pit, yelling orders down at them. Drunken devil that he was. I suppose if I'd been raised as he was, it might turn me a little mean, too. And I'd definitely hate alcohol like Papa did.

Some of Papa's brothers did go bad from their raising. He had one named Hummer, and he wasn't worth the gun-

Making charcoal

powder it would've took to blow him away. He spent three quarters of his life in prison. Hell, he died in prison. Every time he would get out, he would do something stupid like carry some little teenage girl across a state line, and get ten more years for it.

One time he wrote Papa from Georgia, saying, "I'm out of prison and I'd like to come get my life straightened out." And I'll be damned if on his way from Atlanta, Georgia, out to our house he didn't pick him up some cunt, underage. They threw him right back in the slammer again. He just didn't have sense enough to stay on the outside.

One time Hummer did make it to our house, though. Only we were all at church. When we returned in our wagon, Papa saw the car in the driveway, and then a whole stack of bottles and tin cans that had been shot up with a shotgun. Papa walked straight in the front door, into the kitchen, and there was Hummer, sitting at the table. He had Papa's shotgun leaning against a chair and an empty box of shells on the table. I think a box of shotgun shells cost about a dollar back in those days, and Hummer had used up every damn shell Papa had.

"Hello, Colonel," Hummer said brightly. That was Papa's name, Colonel Mareno Allen Loudermilk. "I thought I'd pay you a visit."

Papa didn't say nothing to him at all. He just picked up one of the kitchen chairs and smashed him over the head with it. He whipped him from the kitchen all the way to the front porch and then out into the front yard, just breaking that chair all over him. Then he took up the biggest pieces and kept beating the shit out of him.

And then when Hummer was lying out there in the yard, broken up and bloody, Papa told him, "Don't you never come to my fucking house again."

I'll be a sonofabitch if six weeks later Hummer didn't

come back to visit us again, though. Come back to apologize. When Papa answered the door, he stood there wringing his hands, saying, "I just come to say I'm sorry for wasting that box of shells. I didn't mean nothing by it. I was just waiting for you and got bored."

Papa stepped back in the house and got his shotgun, which he'd loaded from a new box of shells. "Tell you what," Papa said. "If you ever, and I mean ever, show up on my doorstep again, I'll use this box on you."

It hurts a kid to see a thing like that happen. Regardless of what a person does, there ought to be a limit to punishment. But Papa didn't have much of a limit. The size of the crime didn't have much to do with the whipping you'd get. Just a little fuck up could get you beat black and blue. And if you really fucked up, he might just kill you.

When a person's raised hard, stripped away by their father, they tend to do that to their children. Not always, but usually. And our Papa did. It went that way. In some ways, Ira got way more whippings than he needed. And maybe in some other way, he didn't get as many whippings as he needed.

And somewhere along the line, Ira started considering the way he was being treated by Papa. I've always thought he started to weigh the beatings he got against the beatings I got. I don't know if maybe he wondered if there was something wrong with him that wasn't wrong with me, something that only Papa could see. Or maybe he just understood how unfair it was, since most of the trouble we got into, we got into together. He tried not to show it, but there ain't any way in the world he couldn't have held it against me, at least a little.

Either way, I do know that he started to take it real serious. And it never left him.

CHAPTER 4

BREEDING

Papa was a hunting enthusiast. I mean a complete hunting nut. He'd hunt rabbits, squirrels, and especially coons. When he couldn't find nothing else to hunt, he'd even let the dogs tree a possum, if they could find one, and rip it apart. He always said that it was good for the dogs. That once in a while when they treed something, they needed to be able to kill it.

Ira and I also hunted. But we weren't nuts like Papa. It was just a way for us to make a little money. Ed Watkins made a run to Chattanooga every week on Saturdays to buy the supplies he needed to stock his little store, and if Ira and I had any rabbits we'd killed, he'd take them along and sell them for us. I don't think he sold them but for thirty-five cents, but if we sold ten then that was three dollars and fifty cents, which was real money to us.

We shot some rabbits with our old .22 rifle, but most of them we caught using homemade blackgum log traps. The logs were about as big around as your leg, and we'd hollow them out and bore a hole in the end, and then put in a lead loaded up with a trigger. When the rabbit touched that trigger, the lead would fall down behind him, and then he was ours. Every morning before we'd go to school, Ira and I would walk those traps, and when we got one with a rabbit in it, we'd smash its head on a log, field strip it, and hang it in the barn. Then, when Ed Watkins was ready to leave for Chattanooga, we'd throw all of 'em in a burlap bag, and take 'em over to him.

I still have a scar on my hand from one of those rabbits. I reached in to pull it out of a log, and it had turned around somehow and was facing the front. When I stuck my hand in there, the only thing I could get ahold of was that rabbit's head, and when he cleared that log, you talk about scratching. You get ahold of a rabbit like that, you better be stupid and you better have a good hold. I was and I did. That sucker clawed me with his hind feet something terrible, but I never turned him loose. Shit, that was thirty-five cents, I couldn't afford to turn him loose. Of course, Ira was standing there with the .22, and if he had got away from me, Ira would have dropped him. But he didn't need to. I killed that sucker with my hands.

Anyway, like I said, Papa was a real coon hunting nut. And to be a good coon hunter, you need a good coon dog. For one thing, you do all your hunting at night. That's one of the great things about coon hunting. You're out there seeing the world as God made it, in the moonlight, nothing but you and the baying of your dogs. A good coon dog is a special thing. It has to have a good nose, be fast enough to keep up with the raccoon until it can tree it, and tough enough to fight one of the little devils if it gets it cornered. Coons are unbelievably vicious when they get trapped.

Papa prided himself on his dogs. He loved hunting with them, and he loved hearing them bark. He didn't raise a

By a Sand Mountain creek, 1936

whole lot of them, but when he had a real good one he'd try to breed it, and he was successful when he was able. He had some of the best hunting dogs you could find in the state of Alabama.

So, on one occasion, Papa had this bitch in heat that he was real hot to breed, and he'd put her up in the loft of the barn. He wanted to keep her away from the other dogs until he could breed her with this other coonhound that he had his eye on.

Well, Ira and I came down to the barn one day and we saw that pretty much every dog from miles around was circling that barn, sniffing up at her. Naturally, we found the ugliest bulldog we could and we helped him up the old barn ladder into the loft. Coming up behind him, pushing him so he could catch the two rungs with his front paws, then the next two, keeping that up until he got to the top. And when he got up there, he and that coonhound locked together immediately.

Wouldn't you know it, as soon as they started going at it, we heard Papa's truck. He was coming to check on the bitch. Lord, we knew we were dead if we didn't do something quick. We kicked them, hit them, even started pulling on them from opposite ends, but they was hung up. Usually when that happens, you can just leave 'em alone for a while, until the male dog's pecker shrinks and they just fall apart, but we knew we didn't have that kind of time unless we wanted to get killed. So we scrambled around for anything we could think of to get 'em apart.

Finally, Ira grabbed up the bitch's water and threw it on 'em. It worked, but all hell broke loose. That bulldog came after us looking to bite our fucking legs off, and Ira and I had to kick the shit out of him, all the way over the edge of the loft. When he went over, he was still snapping and clawing at the boards, trying to get at us. He landed hard at the bottom and somehow he must've managed to drag his broken ass out of the barn before Papa made it inside. Meanwhile, Ira and I snuck out a hole in the wall and climbed down that way.

Papa never knew that was the day that his hunting dog got ruined, but you should have seen his face when the litter was born. It was just me and him that found the puppies, and he looked like he was gonna be sick. There was no doubt what it was that had got to his hound, the whole litter of little bulldog pups mewling up at us.

"Go get a sack," he said to me, no expression in his voice at all. And when I brought back a burlap sack, he shoved the puppies in it, and handed it to me. "Take them out there to the fencepost," he said.

Well, I knew what he meant. What he meant was take one up, knock its brains out on a fencepost, and then pick up the next one and do the same, until they was all dead. He did that with puppies he had no use for. Papa had no feeling for any animal at all. If it was worthless, then it didn't deserve to eat, and it certainly didn't get none of his food. We had all the pets we wanted as kids, as long as they were outside pets, but he wouldn't allow an animal in the house unless it was a good hunting dog. And if that dog failed, if Papa took it out and it wouldn't hunt, he'd just pick up an ax, say, "Come here, boy," and split its head right down the middle. He wouldn't even consider giving it to someone else. He'd rather kill a useless animal than give it away.

Me, I couldn't take those little bulldog puppies out there and bang their heads against the fencepost. And I couldn't use an ax on them, either. I just didn't have it in me. I wasn't that tough. So I wasted a .22 bullet on each of them. My rabbit hunting bullets. It broke my heart, but I shot each one of those puppies in the head.

That's what I meant when I said you never really did get away with anything with Papa. You always paid some kind of price. When you were dealing with Papa, you were dealing with something inevitable. You couldn't escape him anymore than you could escape winter weather or a hard wind. You could try to hide behind something for a little while, but sooner or later you always had to step out and face it. It didn't do any more good to try to fight him, either. Given the beating you could get for just hesitating, I think he might have killed us if we'd ever tried. Not that we ever did.

The worst thing was that wasn't the first time Ira and I did that, either. We ruined a lot of litters of dogs by mixing them that way. We even killed one of Papa's heifers once. She was in heat, and he knew who he was gonna turn her to, some neighbor's bull. But we also had a bull, almost as big as the barn, way too big for that heifer, and he was sniffing around her. So we waited for Papa to go off somewhere and we put a rope on the cow, backed her into a low place against the fence, and called that bull over. He busted a pecker in her about as long as your arm and killed her graveyard dead right on the spot.

I still don't entirely know why we did those things. Mostly

I think we just wanted to see what would happen, although sometimes I wonder if it was because we enjoyed ruining something we knew Papa took great pride in. He believed in his ability to breed good animals. It was something he liked to talk to other people about, maybe even brag a little, and we created our fair share of breeding disasters for him.

CHAPTER 5

MARY
OF THE
WILD MOOR

Most of the songs Ira and I knew, we learned from Mama. Her name was Georgiane Wootten, though Papa always called her Georgie, and her father was a Baptist preacher. Her people were from a part of the world where a lot of folk songs come from, England, and we learned songs from her that most children wouldn't ever have known. She raised us on those songs, singing them while she worked. And she was always working.

Probably my favorite was "Mary of the Wild Moor." Ira and I learned it while helping her with the housework, before we were old enough to be out in the fields with Papa. Mama knew all those tragic songs, and she loved music. And, of course, anything she loved, we loved. When we were children, the whole world was in her tan face. It was worn before its time, but unlike Papa's, her wrinkles came from laughter.

My mother and father

Ira and I started learning that song just after breakfast one day. After Mama made breakfast for all of us, the kitchen became so unbearably hot from the woodstove that, even with it being cold out, we hung up our flannel coats and moved into the living room. And she taught us the first verse, right there, while she took up her sewing.

It was on one cold wintery night,
When the wind blew across the wild moor,
When Mary came wandering home with her child,
'Till she came to her own father's door.

She taught us that verse to the clacking of the sewing machine. First working on a dress for one of the girls, as it was against Papa's law for the girls to wear britches, and then taking one of the guano bags she'd boiled in lye until it was soft and white, and sewing it into a shirt for Papa.

She stopped working to listen to us try to sing it, correcting us until we had it memorized. And then she let down a quilt she kept hanging on the wall while she taught us the second verse.

Father, dear Father, she cried.
Come down and open the door,
Or the child in my arms will perish and die,
From the winds that blow across the wild moor.

Then she hung up the quilt, and we pulled on our coats and walked with her while she carried water in from the well. It was early in the spring, too early to be warm enough to plant the cotton yet, but the days were warming.

Why did I leave this fair spot,
Where once I was happy and free,
I am now doomed to roam, without friends or a home,
And no one to take pity on me.

Then we followed her out to the meat house for salted pork from one of the hogs that Papa had slaughtered in the autumn. And we stopped by the holes Mama'd dug in the top of the ground and lined with a bed of pine needles during harvest time, so she could retrieve some of the sweet potatoes she'd laid in for the winter.

But her father was deaf to her cry,
Not a sound of her voice did he hear,
So the watchdog did howl, and the village bells tolled,
And the wind blew across the wild moor.

Ira and I carried the pork and vegetables back to the house. Singing the whole time, tottering behind her with our arms full. Mama nodding at us when we got the words right, and shaking her head when, as happened more often than not, we didn't.

Oh, how the old man must have felt,
When he came to the door the next morn,
And he found Mary dead, but the child still alive,
Closely grasping his dead mother's arm.

Inside, the kitchen had cooled off some. After being out in the spring chill, it felt nice. We learned the next verse while helping Mama clean. If you can call it help. We'd be running around her, kicking up the dust she'd gather with her straw broom, making her stop scrubbing to listen to us.

In anguish the old man tore his gray hair,
And the tears down his cheeks they did pour,
When he saw how that night, she had perished and died,
From the winds that blew across the wild moor.

Then Mama began to cook supper. Lord, she could cook. She ran the house, just as Papa ran the outside work. He didn't tell her how to cook a meal, and she didn't tell him how much wood to chop so that we could get through the winter. It was a good setup. I don't actually recall but one or two loud conversations, where it was obvious even to a kid that they wasn't agreeing on something. Through them, I came to believe even then that if you take care of your corner of life, you'll find a partner that will take care of theirs, and then you'll have a long and happy togetherness. Otherwise, you'll fight all the time.

In grief the old man pined away,
And the child to its mother went soon.
And no one they say has lived there to this day,
And the cottage to ruin has gone.

When we'd grabbed the sweet potatoes from outside, I'd gotten a little hopeful that Mama would make a sweet potato cobbler for after dinner. And, sure enough, that's exactly what she began working on. Womenfolk of the twenty-first century will look at you like you're crazy if you bring up a sweet potato cobbler. "I've never heard of anything like that," they'll say. But they do exist, and have for a long time. It's made precisely like a peach, apple, or blackberry cobbler, and, as far as I'm concerned, it's one of the best desserts I've ever tasted.

It was then, while she was working on that cobbler that Ira and I tried the whole song, all the way through. Closing with the last verse, which we'd been practicing while she was preparing the sweet potatoes.

> *But the villagers point out the spot,*
> *Where the willows grow over the door.*
> *Saying there Mary died, once the gay village bride,*
> *From the wind that blew across the wild moor.*

Like I said, that's the saddest song I've ever sung. It's supposed to be a true song, too. And I believe it. Back when I was boy, if a girl got pregnant, she never did return home. Not pregnant and single. She just wasn't welcome. Sometimes we'd notice one of these girls missing, and being children, we'd ask, "Where's Mary?"

The grown-ups would always have the same answer, "She's off to college."

Even as kids we knew better. These people were just like us, so poor they did good to get a kid through grade school, let alone college. So if they said they sent one to college, it's a sure bet she wasn't never coming back, not unless she had a husband. And then only after many years.

The problem in the song was that Mary was brave enough to come back home. You'll notice that the song says "her father was deaf to her cry." Not deaf, but deaf to her cry. It wasn't that he couldn't hear her, he just wouldn't hear her. He laid up there on his big featherbed and let her freeze to death. And the child, too.

It was the first song I learned, but I can't hardly sing it now, because it's so possible. Because it happened then, and it could still happen now. And nobody should be that cruel, not to a child.

It was about the time that Ira and I finished memorizing the song that Papa and our older sister came in from whatever work they were doing. Our sister's name was Charlsey. My Mama and Papa took turns naming us kids, and my Mama's Papa was named Charlie, so she wanted more than anything else for her first child to be named after him. Well lo and behold, the first was born a girl and Mama couldn't exactly name her Charlie. But she got as close as she could with Charlsey. That seemed to soothe her, and then Papa named the second baby, which was Ira. And then along I came, and since I was born on grandpa's birthday, I naturally got the name Charlie.

We all sat down for dinner. It was pork and Irish potatoes and corn bread. We hardly ever could afford flour to make biscuits, but there was always corn bread. And after dinner, we had the sweet potato cobbler I'd been waiting on.

Then, when we'd cleaned up, Mama asked Papa, "Would you like to see what Charlie and Ira learned today?"

"What'd they learn?" Papa asked.

"Go ahead," Mama said. "Show him."

So we stood right there in the living room and sang "Mary of the Wild Moor" for Papa. A song that had been carried across an ocean by Mama's people, and passed down to us, just like it had been passed down to her, almost like we were singing with all their ghosts down the generations. That was how we learned to sing. It's something you can't teach and you can't fake, and I'm afraid it has been all but lost forever.

And you could tell by watching Papa that he was listening to every note, that he really enjoyed it. We were so proud that we never could have imagined a time would come when we'd almost resent singing for him.

CHAPTER 6

SACRED HARP

Papa probably loved music as much as we did. After working in the fields all day, he'd pick up his banjo and do three or four songs most every night. And whenever time allowed, he'd invite family and friends to the house, and everybody would bring their instrument along and have a song to sing, a story to tell. That was one extremely enjoyable part of growing up in what you might call a desolate area.

He was pretty proud that Ira and I could sing like we did, too. Papa could pick a good claw hammer banjo, but he didn't sing in public. It got so that when company would come over, we weren't even allowed to leave the room until we'd sung a couple of songs.

It started with our Uncle Verlon. He was one of Papa's brothers who lived not too far away in Rome, Georgia, and he'd come down to play music. He had this doohickey around his neck with a harp in it, and he'd play the guitar at the same time, singing his way through the song while Papa played, and then, when he came to the turnaround, blowing the harp. He was something else to watch.

One night after they finished playing, Papa said, "I'll tell you what, Verlon, you oughta see what my boys can do."

Well, Ira and I knew what that meant, so we started sidling for the door.

"Now, wait a minute," Papa said. "You can sing Uncle Verlon a song or two."

We must have looked like we were terrified, because Uncle Verlon chuckled a little and said, "I do believe they're bashful, Colonel." He was right, too. And it didn't help that both his kids, our cousins, were right there, and barely able to hold in their giggles.

In those days, there was a bed in every room of the house except the kitchen, and the one in our living room was one of those old-style, steel-frame types that was built at least two feet off the floor. "Ain't nobody ever died of being bashful," Papa said. "Tell you what, boys, if you're that nervous, crawl under the bed here where we can't see you, and do your singing there."

So Ira and I crawled under the bed, and from there we sang "Mary of the Wild Moor" with our tails together, facing opposite directions. We must've done a good job, too, because the room was pretty much dead silent when we finished. No giggling or chuckling at all. Still, we didn't give Papa a chance to ask for another one. We slid down to the end of the bed, and then ran like hell out the front door.

We were screwed after that, though. Once Papa'd figured out that trick for us, we had to sing from under the bed pretty much anytime anybody stopped by the house. And if we went any place, he expected us to sing at the drop of a hat. Just walking down the road, Papa'd pop his fingers and say, "Do 'em one," and that's the way it was. We'd do at least one song, even if that's all we had time for. Papa saw to it.

Lord, we hated him for making us sing like that. But as always with Papa, there was probably more to it than what we saw. He worked in ways you couldn't always figure out at first, and as much as we got pissed off at having to sing, he trained all the bashfulness right out of us. By making us sing those songs for folks, he forced us to learn how to perform. And we began to understand that we could entertain folks.

That summer was also the first time we were allowed to sing with everybody at the Haynes' reunion. That was my maternal grandmother's name, Haynes, and her people were known all over for their Sacred Harp singing. My grandmother started that reunion, and it's still going on today, more than one hundred and thirty years later.

To get us there on time, Papa got us out of bed just after midnight and loaded us in the wagon. Ira, I, and Charlsey were all still sleepy, huddling together in the wagon to keep warm. We rolled up to Shady Grove, Alabama, around eight o'clock in the morning. The reunion was in this little shotgun church. A little porch on front, a straight back, an outhouse around back.

We were early, but Papa had brought a homemade wagon so we'd have something to play with. It was nothing but wheels he'd cut from a pine tree and fixed with an iron axle and then finished with an old tarp, but we loved playing with it. We played around in the grass, trying not to get our nice clothes dirty as we watched the people arrive. Everybody wore their nicest clothes. Most of them only had one good suit, but they'd have it on every time you'd see them there.

Finally, it got to around nine o'clock and everybody was called into the church. We all filed in and sat down in the pews, which were arranged around an open space in the middle. A Sacred Harp church ain't like most churches. They don't have any instruments, not even a piano. As soon as everybody made their way inside, the leader, who was this

Shady Grove Baptist Church, 1936

guy from Ider with a perfect ear, shouted out somebody's name. Then that person stood up with their immediate family and walked to the middle, where they called out what song they was gonna sing, usually by page number from the songbook. Then the leader sang out the notes and gave a hum for the pitch, and we all stood up and laid into it.

That first song was electric. The whole church filled with the music of our voices. This was the first time I was really expected to sing along, but I joined in as easily as if I'd been doing it a hundred years. The human voice, that's what they're talking about when they say Sacred Harp, and there's nothing like it in the world. You can't really record it, either. Since everybody sings, it's awful hard to get a microphone positioned so you can mix all of them. But it does your soul good to hear it.

We sang until eleven thirty or so, and then some of the

womenfolk started getting up and sliding out the front door of the church, leaving the men and children. I snuck a look over at Ira and his face was as happy as I knew mine was. The women sneaking out meant only one thing. They were going out to their wagons to get the food to set on that big long table.

Finally, the song leader called lunch, and me and Ira all but ran out of the church, where we found Mama and asked her to fill our plates, because we were too small to reach. Then we found a patch of grass and sat down with our food. The adults talking about who was here last year, who ain't here now, who died, and who got married.

We kept our mouths full of food right up until about a quarter to one, when the ladies started putting the stuff away in their baskets, and Papa stood up and said, "Well, boys, it's about time." Then we followed the menfolk inside, where we sang a song or two until the women could be free of their chores, joining their voices with the men.

It was late in the afternoon that our turn came, the song leader calling out, "Okay, Georgiane Loudermilk, you and your family."

All of a sudden, my legs starting shaking and I couldn't breathe. There was something about walking through all those people, up to the center of the church, which turned my lungs into ice. I started to see spots, I was so scared.

"I can't do it without you, Charlie," Mama said warmly. She, Ira, and Charlsey were already all standing, waiting for me.

"I can't," I said.

"It's an honor to get up with your mother and help her sing that song," Papa said.

"I can't do it," I said again. I pinched my hands between my legs.

"You will do it," Papa said. "You make me beg you to get up there, and you'll feel the welts after this reunion."

"Come on, Charlie," said Ira. And as scared as I was,

I looked up at him. He was smiling down at me, confident and tall. And that was the thing about Ira, as much as he could convince me to do something I knew I shouldn't do, like chop down that damn persimmon tree, he could always help me on the path to something that needed doing. There was two sides to his gift for convincing, as there was two sides to everything with him.

So I nodded and stood. My legs were still shaking, but taking courage from him, I stood and started walking. Then I stopped and looked back at Papa, who was still sitting in the pew. "Ain't you coming, Papa?" I asked.

"I ain't no singer," he said. "I'll enjoy listening to y'all right here."

Well, that didn't make a whole lot of sense to me. Especially since he'd just promised me a whipping if I didn't get up and sing. But I knew better than to argue. So I followed Ira down to the center of the church, and helped him and Charlsey sing two songs for Mama. Mama didn't even bother with a songbook. She knew every note and every word to every song in there. They were all in her head. And because she'd taught them to us, we knew them, too.

As soon as we finished, there was this girl there, just a little bit older than Ira and I, and when she got up with her family and started to sing, it was like nothing else we'd ever heard. She sang her part way up in the treetops, and then, just when you thought no human being could go any higher, her voice swooped down like a bird from the treetops, ran along the floor with us, and then soared again. It gave me chills.

When I looked over at Ira to see if he was noticing it, I realized right away that I better not pester him. He was studying her so intently it made you uncomfortable to see. But that's the way he was. Any time there was music anywhere, he stopped and paid attention. You could almost see his brain working it over, picking it apart, trying to figure out why every piece was in its place.

That was another of Ira's gifts. You could play him a piece of music and he could take it down to its parts, pull out what he needed, and use it. He could do it with people, too. That's why he was so good with women, even at an early age. He wasn't ever as good-looking as he thought he was, but he could see right into them. Unfortunately, it wasn't always a gift for the rest of us. As surely as he could pinpoint something he could take advantage of, he could spot a weakness. And if he wanted to, he could take your flesh down to the bone with it.

Sure enough, from then on after he saw that girl, there'd come a time when we were singing together that he'd slip into one of those high parts and then come back down, just like she did. He built it right into our act.

In a way, our entire career was built on doing unorthodox things like that, things no sensible person might do, and we learned a lot of them from Sacred Harp. Sometimes the tenor and the melody would work together, and I would go down as Ira went up, and we would end up in the same place, only he would be twice as high as I would be, and we got so many compliments on it that we started using it fairly regular.

It baffled a lot of people, too, how we could change parts without nudging or winking at each other. He'd take the high lead and I'd do the low harmony under it, and he knew exactly when my part would get too high for me just like I knew when his would get too low for him, and we could change in the middle of a word.

Part of the reason we could do that was that we'd learned to have a good ear for other peoples' voices when we sang Sacred Harp. But the other part is that we were brothers. There's no one that knows your weaknesses like a brother. I knew Ira's, and, as he proved time and time again in our career, he surely knew mine.

CHAPTER 7

DUMB

It was a hard life growing up on a cotton farm. Ira and I watched the way Papa worked, and we knew the way he worked all of us kids. And I think we got to thinking he was pretty dumb. He'd made some pretty stupid choices to end up where he was. We got to thinking that way a lot, I suppose. When we thought of all the things a person could be in their lives, we couldn't think of nothing worse than being a cotton farmer.

It also occurred to us that if you were gonna be a cotton farmer, Sand Mountain might be one of the dumbest places in the world to do it. Ira and I hadn't really been anywhere yet, but we knew there were places where the land was wide open, like Texas or Arkansas, where it might make sense to farm cotton. But there weren't no huge hundred-acre fields around us. There was just hills. You'd have a twenty-five acre field, and then you'd have that much woods again.

Beyond that, the government would only let him grow

Picking cotton

a little of it. He was allowed to grow just five acres each year, and that wasn't nearly enough to live on. But somewhere along the line, somebody'd invented a cotton gin that could take bolls of cotton that hadn't opened all the way, and Papa would buy up the fields around us where those bolls hadn't been picked. It might be a twenty acre field that only had two bales of cotton in it, but he'd put us kids in there, and in a day and a half he'd expect us to have everything picked. Those bolls brought less money than the top grade, but it was money. Papa'd keep us working well into the winter most years that way. He'd only let up around Christmas time, when it was so cold you couldn't hardly do your job.

Ira and I hated it. All of it. And I don't know if Papa caught on that we were feeling that he was stupid, but he cured us of it. One year he waited until the cotton field got just as white and thick as snow, and then, just after we'd eaten breakfast round sunrise, he opened the door and stuck his head in from outside. "You three oldest," he said, "come with me."

Ira, Charlsey, and I jumped right up and followed him outside to the cotton field without hesitating. We knew that if you didn't move when Papa said to move, you were more than likely to get a whipping, so we ran trying to keep up, almost running into his backside when he stopped at the edge of the cotton field and stood looking out over it. It looked like a white blanket thrown across our whole five acres. He asked us, "You see all that cotton?"

We all nodded in unison and said, "Yessir." And we even managed to put some enthusiasm in it. Even though we weren't too happy about the beginning of picking season, about knowing that we were about to be worked like dogs in the field, we knew better than to show it.

Then, standing out there before all that cotton, Papa did something he'd never done before. Without looking away from the field, he reached into the pocket of his overalls, pulled out a five-dollar bill, and held it up in the air. "You see this?"

This time we were a little more enthusiastic when we said, "Yessir." We had some idea where this was going.

He stuck the bill back in his pocket. "I'm gonna give it to whichever of you can pick the most cotton today," he said.

Well, back then a five-dollar bill was about equal to what a hundred dollars would be today. So we hit those rows of cotton at a dead run. And as soon as our cotton sack got full, we ran it back to the wagon as fast as we could, emptied it, and got right back to picking. We worked like raving idiots, never even looking up from the cotton rows.

It's an art, really, picking cotton. You can't do it in a terrible rush if you want to do it right. You only pick it when the boll opens up completely, and then your hand will fit right on the five locks of cotton. But there are burrs that stick out at the end, and your hand's likely to be as bloody as if you've been fighting a pit bull by the end of the day, even if you're careful. And that day we were going at it in a fever, taking no care at all how we picked the bolls. We worked our hands until they were completely ruined.

And then, when it was too dark to pick anymore, Papa called us over. We hadn't bothered with lunch or a break of any kind, and we were completely worn down to nothing, falling asleep on our feet. We all just stood there rocking on our heels and bleeding from our hands, while Papa silently tallied up the cotton each of us had picked, the sun sinking behind him.

When he was done, he turned to Charlsey, standing there in her homemade dress, and he said, "Okay, Charlsey, I got down here how much you picked," and he showed her the tally. Then he turned to Ira. "And Ira, here's how much you picked." And then he looked at me, held up the tally, and said, "And you won the five dollars, Charlie." And just as he said he would, he gave me the five-dollar bill.

I had figured I'd won, but I was still pretty happy. Some people are just naturally better at picking cotton than others. The cotton stalk never grows over thirty inches tall, and you have to pick it from top to bottom, so tall people have a handicap because they have to stoop. Ira was tall, but I was just five foot and five inches, and I didn't have to bend over very much to reach from the top of the stalk to the ground. It was something I could be better at than Ira, something that came easy to me. It probably wasn't fair, but I was proud that I was that much a better picker than he was.

But then, when I'd gotten over my excitement a little, I noticed that Papa was still standing there, looking down at his tally sheet, as if he was memorizing it. And I started to get the uneasy feeling that something else was coming.

"Now, I'll tell you something else," Papa said, finally. "I know exactly what each of you can pick." He looked up from the sheet. "And if you miss that mark tomorrow, I'll have a completely different surprise for you."

So we got out there every day that picking season, the whole season, working just like we had that first day. We never took a breather. We just put our heads down and ran at those rows, showing him every day how much we could pick.

That's what Papa expected of his kids. And he expected it of us every day. As a farm boy, you learn what you need to do pretty quick when it comes to work. If given the chance, I don't think I'd take five million dollars for all I learned picking cotton. But if I had that kind of money, I'd gladly give five million dollars to keep from having to go through it again.

I can guarantee you that Papa worked the girls just as hard as he worked the boys, too. That was necessary in those days. By the time you hired help, you wouldn't make nothing on your crop, so you had to work your kids. That's why most all my sisters got married young. They felt like they was being used by my daddy for slaves. And they were.

My oldest sister, Charlsey, I'm sure she married before she was fifteen. By her eighteenth birthday, she had four sons and lost one daughter at birth. Another of my sisters also got married when she was fifteen years old. Ran off and eloped. And then another of 'em liked the sound of that so much, she hunted down her boyfriend and eloped, too, and she was only thirteen.

They were too young to be getting married, but I guess they couldn't see any other way to get away from Papa's forced labor. The funny thing being that it wasn't any easier on them when they did get married. They got worked just as hard bringing in their husband's crops.

Papa was really disappointed with them. He was sure

they must be pretty dumb. We talked about it once, just after the thirteen-year-old ran off. We were out working, chopping wood, and he was fuming over it. He was just breaking the hell out of that wood, sending chunks flying all over the place. "How about you, Charlie?" he said, between swings. "I bet you'll probably get married next? Sometime before the year's out?"

"No, I won't," I said, gathering up the wood. That was my job, to gather it up and pile it. I hated doing it when he was mad, too, because I had to gather it all the way from twenty or thirty feet away from his chopping stump.

"I'll bet you will," he said again. "You ain't got no more sense than your sisters."

"All right, Papa, I'll take that bet," I said. "How old was you when you got married?"

"I was twenty-two years old," he said. "And I knew what I was doing."

Sure you did, I thought. And I'm not dumb enough to end up with your life, either. But I didn't say anything. I just took note of that number, twenty-two, and I knew I'd never get married any younger than that.

Anyway, we worked the whole rest of that season from sunup until sundown. We worked until it was too dark to work, and then stumbled down to the house and rinsed our bloody hands down with rubbing alcohol, so they'd be ready to use again the next day. Because at the end of every day, Papa would show each of us that tally and say, "You'll do that every day, or you'll get your ass whipped."

So who was the dumb one? It sure wasn't Papa.

But being worked liked that, meeting Papa's tallies, set us on the path of music just as much as our love of singing did. For Ira especially. One night, while climbing into bed, bone-tired after another day of picking, he said to me, "We ain't got no choice, Charlie. You know that."

"No choice about what, Ira?" I said. I already had the blanket up to my chin and I could hardly keep my eyes open.

"No choice about whether or not we make it as singers." His voice sounded choked up, and I looked over at him. He was older than me, almost full grown, but he looked like he might just bust out in tears. "I can't do this for the rest of my life."

"I know, Ira," I said.

And I did. I probably didn't understand how much his back hurt from having to stoop over to keep up with the picking. Nor did I know what it felt like to be the oldest, to take Papa's beatings the way he did. But I knew what he meant. That having a music career didn't mean the Opry or riding around in a fancy automobile anymore.

It meant not picking cotton for the rest of our lives. It meant survival.

CHAPTER 8

BROOM STRAWS

No matter how hard we worked, the cotton fields never brought in enough money to support us, and Papa always had to find other ways to make money. He had a blacksmith's shop for one thing, or a shed, anyway, with an old-time grindstone for sharpening things. It ran on part of a car tire, which also operated the bellows, and one of us kids had to turn it while he was working.

That was where I learned to smoke. All the dudes out there getting work done would just flip their cigarettes down, and most of them wouldn't even be half smoked. And since back in those days none of the cigarettes had filters on them, Ira and I would go out where they tossed them, and we were tough enough that we could put our big toe on the coal and snuff them out. Then we'd pick them up, do what the Army would call fieldstrip them, breaking the tobacco out of the papers, and put it in a little sack. We had Chesterfields, Lucky Strikes, Camels, Pall Malls, whatever the guys were smoking.

Still smoking 78 years later

And when we got enough tobacco together, we'd wander off and get some brown paper sacks, chew the edge up, and roll us some cigarettes. I was only five when I learned to roll a cigarette. I had to, because nobody would help me.

Another thing Papa did was to sell vegetables. We had an acre vegetable garden, and when spring came we would gather up whatever vegetables we could in the afternoon and load 'em up in our old two-horse, steel-wheel wagon about sundown. Then, at two o'clock the next morning, Papa would wake us up and say, "Which one of you boys wants to ride to Fort Payne with me?"

"I do," I'd say. It was usually me who wanted to go. I can't imagine anything Ira'd rather do less than ride four hours in a wagon with Papa. So I'd help him hitch the mules up to the wagon, hang an oil lantern on the back for a tail light, and we'd start to Fort Payne. It was twenty-one miles, and if you kept the mules stepping good, you could get there by about six or seven o'clock in the morning, which was exactly the time the grocery stores would open.

We'd hit every store we could. Me carrying one bushel, him carrying two. It wouldn't take us more than an hour to sell it all, and then we'd unhook the mules from where he'd tied them, and he'd back them up a little, turn them around, and, with good luck, we would be home before noon. That was what we lived on until the big crops came in. The cotton, corn, and beans, all that.

Once Papa got a truck, it got a little easier. He stopped driving the vegetables into Fort Payne, and started traveling to this curb market in Knoxville, Tennessee, where he could ask better prices. There was no traffic on the street, and he'd back up the vehicle so it was hanging over the sidewalk, and people could look at whatever he had to sell in the bed.

Knoxville was a long way from our house, so Papa didn't get home until late, but we always waited up for him. And

Market Square, Knoxville

one night we got the surprise of our lives. It was about one o'clock in the morning, and he walked in the door with his hands full of old records. Six or seven of them. It turned out there was a record shop on that street with the curb market.

We wasted no time running them up to our room, where we kept the graphophone. My Lord, there was the Blue Sky Boys, the Monroe Brothers, Roy Acuff, and the Delmore Brothers. We were bustin' to hear both sides of every record. And even with it being so late, Papa let us listen to four or five songs before he hollered, "All right, boys, knock it off. I need to get some sleep."

In some way, I think Papa knew what music meant to us. He was a cotton farmer because it was what he knew. And there's no doubt he could be hard on us, but I think he also steered us to music as much as he knew how to. He was a private man, and he didn't explain the reasons for the things he did, but I can't see any other reason for him to bring us those albums.

Anyway, there was no chance of us sleeping that night. We'd have rather died in our sleep than be in a room with an unlistened record like that. So we huddled up in our blankets against the night chill, and just stared at the old graphophone.

Then I heard Ira's breath catch. And I knew exactly what that meant. "I got an idea," he whispered to me, and I felt my breath freeze up in my chest, knowing I was about to be convinced of something. "Can you sneak downstairs to the kitchen?"

"You know I can," I whispered back. "As long as Papa's asleep."

"All right," he whispered. "Here's what you do. I want you to sneak down there and pull some broom straws."

"Broom straws?"

"Broom straws. Just pull 'em out of the broom."

"What are you fixing to do with broom straws?" I was completely flummoxed.

"I'll tell you what I'm gonna do as soon as you go fetch 'em," he said.

Well, I shrugged and did what he asked. Which is what I always did, I guess. I snuck down to the living room door, and listened until I heard Papa snoring, and then I tiptoed into the kitchen, and yanked five or six straws out of the broom.

Ira was cranking the graphophone when I got back. I almost had a heart attack. "What are you doing?" I whispered.

"I ain't gonna put the needle down. Hand me one of those broom straws."

I gave him one, and then watched as he put one end in his teeth, and put the other on the record, just like it was the needle. "It works," he said, forgetting to whisper. "Give it a try." So I did the same on the other side of the record, and sure enough, I could hear the music in my head as plain as could be through those broom straws.

I don't know how Ira came up with that idea, but it was one of the most amazing things I'd ever seen. He'd do that sometimes, come up with an idea that you wouldn't think nobody in their right mind could ever come up with, and sure enough it'd work. And then, when you'd ask him about it, he either wouldn't or couldn't tell you where it come from. Ira was like Papa in some ways, and that was one. For all the talking, charming, and blustering he could do, he kept most of his thoughts to himself.

Of course, not all of those old records played so well after we listened to them like that a few times with the broom straws. And Papa used to get awful angry at that guy in Knoxville who always sold him all them scratched records. But it worked, and you can bet we listened to both sides of every album every night he brought a few home.

CHAPTER 9

SINGING SCHOOL

Once Ira and I really set our sights on a music career, I all but gave up on school. I made it through grade school, but the only reason I did is because we used to have this thing every Friday at noon where the teacher would open the sliding partition between the two rooms, and all the students would spend the rest of the day singing songs and playing their instruments. Ira and I loved that. Every Friday we'd get up there and sing whatever songs we was working on until it was time for school to let out, and we never said a word about it to Papa or Mama.

Neither Ira nor I had any instruments at the time, but Papa had a real nice five-string banjo. On Friday mornings, I'd go out the front door and make sure Papa was in the barn, and then Ira would take the banjo and cut out the back door and walk across the field where Papa couldn't see him. Then about a mile down toward the school, he'd come back in to the road where I was and we'd walk in together.

We did that for the bigger part of two years. But one morning, Papa come out the front of the barn, and saw Ira behind the house. It was flat country, and you had to get a hundred and fifty feet from the house before you couldn't be seen. Papa put two and two together. He didn't even bother asking us, "What're you doing with my banjo?" neither. He just went down to the school and told the teacher, "When you're finished with my boys, you send 'em home right away. I need them to work in the fields." And then he told us that if we ever snuck out of the house with his banjo again, he'd give us a whipping we'd never forget. That pretty much did away with any interest I had in school. I didn't make it past the ninth grade.

I don't know if Papa felt bad about doing that or if he just wanted some control over our singing, but that summer when we were between planting and picking time, he got it in his head that it was time to develop our musical talent. Back then, they had these wandering singing teachers that were about half con artist, making their living traveling town to town, giving lessons. Well, one had stopped by our house and told Papa, "Even if a boy can sing good, he can't do nothing with it if he doesn't have any idea what he's singing. You send them to me, and I'll teach them everything they need to know."

"What exactly are you planning to teach them?" Papa asked him.

"I'll teach them how to read music," the teacher said. "When they're done, they'll be able to walk into any church in the country, pick up a songbook, and sing any song in it."

"All right," Papa said. "How much?"

"Ten dollars each. But that's ten dollars for two whole weeks of singing school. You won't find a better deal than that anywhere."

Even at a dollar a day that money was hard to come by.

Still, Papa thought it would be good for us, so he promised this guy that he'd send us that year. And sure enough, when the time came, Papa gave each of us ten dollars to pay the man, and sent us off the three miles to the church where they were holding the school.

Neither Ira nor I understood how *Fa, So, La, Ti, Do* could help us get on the Opry or ride in an air-cooled Franklin. And reading music was just nonsense in our minds. We knew what we were trying to sing. But we started out to the school, and once we got down the road a little ways, we ran into the Peek twins. They called 'em Big 'Un and Little 'Un, and they were two of our best friends. Their parents had been talked into sending them to singing school, too, even though they had no musical ability at all. So we joined them, walked down the road a little over a quarter of a mile, and came to Ed Watkins' store.

Everything we needed came from Ed Watkins' store, and it was a place of wonder to me. I loved it when Papa would send me to buy something. I'd pass the tobacco chewers and snuff dippers out front doing their business in the dirt where Mrs. Watkins couldn't run them out of the store with a broom, and the first thing I'd see would be those bushels of apples, those red delicious apples, and you could just see the juice running out of them before you got your hand on them. And then the enclosed glass counter with all imagines of candy, from peppermints to chocolate pieces to lemon drops. I'd just sit and stare at them.

The most embarrassing thing in my life, though, was when Papa would tell me to go to the store and ask Mr. Watkins to charge something. I'd rather have taken a whipping. Even as a child, I knew that Watkins had so many charge accounts that he had trouble paying for the stuff he had to buy to put back in the store. It was a wonder he didn't go broke with so many of us buying on credit, only paying him off when we gathered in our crops. He never complained about it, though. And if Mama had a hen that quit laying, he'd buy it from her. He'd buy whole chickens, or he'd buy eggs, and that helped us out a lot between picking seasons.

Well, we should have passed that store and kept going. But I think I knew before anybody that we weren't going to. Because as soon as I realized we were getting close, I knew I wasn't gonna be strong enough to resist the temptation. I've always had a sweet tooth, and all that candy just started dancing in front of my eyes. And with it, all those packages of ready-rolled cigarettes. I knew how good those were compared to the ones we rolled out of brown paper sacks.

Then, about fifty yards from the store, I noticed that everybody else had stopped talking, too. And they all had the same look on their face that I imagined I did. A lost and dreamy look as we all realized how much candy and cigarettes we could each buy with ten dollars.

Ira cleared his throat. "I suppose it wouldn't hurt to stop and take a look. Just to see what we could buy if we wanted to."

"Naw, that couldn't hurt nobody," Big 'Un chimed in immediately.

Neither Little 'Un nor I said anything. I don't know about him, but I think I was about to faint from the excitement.

Once we got inside, all pretense of just looking disappeared completely. We walked out with all the cigarettes and candy bars we could carry, and then snuck off in the woods and had a ball all day, eating candy, smoking, messing around. Come evening time we left in plenty of time to get us back to the house before Papa.

Well, Papa knew right away what we'd done. Which shouldn't have surprised us. It seemed like there wasn't a thing in the world he didn't know. So the first thing he asked us when we walked in the door was, "How'd you boys like that singing school?"

"We liked it just fine, Papa," Ira said.

"Good," he said. "Good. What'd you learn?"

"We learned notes," I said. "Fa, So, La, Ti, Do."

"Good, good. Did you learn to read any music?"

"Some," Ira said.

"A little bit," I said.

"Good, good," he said. Then he just stood there looking at us for a minute. "You got any of that money left?"

He knew. And he didn't bother waiting for an answer, he just beat the holy shit out of both of us, right there. I'll tell you, it wasn't worth the fun we had in the woods to get that whipping.

It might have helped us some to learn to read music, to tell the truth. But we never did. Once we started to make money, my brother bought a little wire recorder, and if he came across a good melody and some good words, he would record it. Hank Williams had one of them, too. It probably would have been easier if we could just write our songs out, but that wasn't the way it worked out.

Even so, I'm still glad Ira and I did what we did. It might have ruined us if we'd went to that school. We got the music bug early, and once you get the bug, it's in your blood. It won't let you be at ease, it won't let you relax, not if you're trying to do anything else. The worst thing that could have happened to us would have been to be cured of it by school.

CHAPTER 10

FLYING JENNY

If we were going to make a career out of music, Ira knew that we needed to start performing more than just when Papa told us to. We had to get out in front of people. The problem was that neither Ira nor I had any instruments. So we found a boy named Lonnie Justice who had a guitar, and he furnished the music while we did the singing. Lonnie even sounded a little like Mother Maybelle Carter when he played. Of course, back then everybody who could pick up a guitar could play "Wildwood Flower" if they played any country music at all. But Lonnie really had some talent.

Every time you work at what you want to do, you learn something. If you want to make it in music, you'll work not just because you're making a little money, but because you're learning. I still believe that today, and I had to back then, because we never made any money to speak of. Starting out, we'd work for free at anything anybody would let us.

We worked a lot of cake walks, for one thing. They don't

have those today, but back then, all the pretty girls in the area would bake a cake for menfolk to bid on, and whoever bid the highest would get to sit down and eat it with the girl who baked it. It was a popular sport in our neck of the woods, and we played all of them we could.

We also played every dance we could find. A big part of my youth was spent standing in the corner while everyone else was dancing and having fun. But if you make music, you have to make it when the people want it, and if the fun is all over by the time you get through playing, that's just tough shit.

We were honing the act that would carry us through the rest of our career. We were rawboned skinny, and our outfits were hand-me-downs, but it was coming together. Ira was the taller of us, and he took the role of leader and master of cer-

Ira and Charlie Louvin

You'll LOVE THOSE LOUVIN BROTHERS Singing "I WISH YOU KNEW"

emonies. He had a quick tongue and the kind of hard, dark good looks that the girls fell for. I could hold my own, but I was shorter and blond, and I never had the interest in taking the lead the way he did. For me, it was more about the music.

We didn't have any records out, of course, so we did other people's songs. There was a Delmore Brothers' tune, "Freight Train Boogie," that we liked doing. They also wrote a lot of songs about Sand Mountain, and since that's where we were born and raised, we did those too. We also did the Blue Sky Boys and Monroe Brothers. Anything we liked that we could put harmony to.

But then, just as we were getting rolling, playing every weekend, even it was for free, Lonnie got married. And, as so often happens, his wife made him totally undependable. Every night she'd tell him whether he could go out or not, and most times she said no, because she didn't want him traipsing all over the county without her. Well, we just couldn't stand for that. If everybody in the band tried to bring their wife with them, the first thing you know you'd have to buy two or three new cars just to haul 'em all. Not that we had any cars at the time, but we understood the principle.

Lonnie's quitting didn't stop us, though. Ira went and traded an old bicycle he had for a beat up guitar, and we kept playing. That arrangement worked pretty well for a while, too, but then Ira came to me one day to have a talk. I was outside on the porch of our old house, not much more than fourteen years old, and he sat down next to me and cleared his throat.

"Uh oh," I said. "I know what that means."

"Charlie," he said. "You're gonna have to learn to play the guitar."

Well, I would have rather somebody pissed down my leg than told me something like that. "I don't want to," I said, hanging my head.

"It's necessary, Charlie," he said. "The Blue Sky Boys got a mandolin and a guitar, the Monroe Brothers got a mandolin and a guitar, the Delmore Brothers got a tenor guitar and a regular guitar. I'm gonna take up the mandolin, and I need you to take up the guitar."

He was right. There was no getting around it. Every duet had what you'd call a lead instrument and a rhythm instrument. And since there was only the two of us, it wasn't too hard to figure out who was talented enough to play the lead instrument.

So we went to a pawnshop in Chattanooga where he found an F5 mandolin and I found a Gibson guitar, and we bought 'em on a payment plan. Mine was just as black as a telephone, and a pretty good little guitar, too. Ira taught me all the chords he knew, and the rest I learned on my own.

They were good instruments. Not the best, but good. Ira was the one who insisted that we didn't buy the cheapest. He

With some of my guitars

was right about that. If you're ever gonna be anything, you have to act like you're already something. You have to have good instruments and pretty nice clothing, and the rest of it'll take care of itself if you have any talent.

God only knows how long it took Ira to become proficient on the mandolin. It's a tricky little instrument. And me, I was scared to death to start on the guitar. I'd heard a bunch of good guitar players, and I knew I wasn't in their league. But it turned out that I didn't need to be. As I figured out, all the guitar player really has to do is hang on, and it wasn't too long before I was holding up my end. I even got to where I enjoyed the duets more, since I was putting a little more into them.

And just then, after we bought those instruments, we got something we never thought we'd get. Our first paying gig. I'll never forget it as long as I live. It was a Fourth of July celebration in Flat Rock, Alabama. A nice little fair in this small town right in the middle of a farming community. The town probably only had thirty or forty people inside the city limits, but everybody had farms around there, so there was quite a crowd. Folks turned out in their Sunday best. They had cotton candy and popcorn, gifts you could buy, and all kinds of carnival games you could play to win prizes.

They also had a Flying Jenny, which was a kind of mule-drawn merry-go-round. It had benches, like church pews, curved around a center post, and folks would sit on them while the mules walked around, pulling those that paid to ride. And, like all rides, it needed music, which was where we came in. We set up right in the middle against the post, and played every song we knew, turning right along with the people who were riding. Every three songs, the driver would stop the mules, and they'd file everybody off, load up a new batch, and start the mules again. That's all you'd get for fifteen cents, three songs. We played the whole day, with a short break every forty-five minutes. Just long enough for us to buy an orange juice, drink it, and then throw it up before we had to get back on again.

At the end of the day, the man gave us fifty dollars apiece. Fifty dollars for me and fifty dollars for Ira. I could hardly believe it when he handed that fifty dollar bill to me, but I stuck it in my pocket like it was something I'd done a hundred times before.

That night I couldn't sleep. I tossed and turned in my bed in the room I shared with Ira, thinking of all the things that cost fifty dollars that I'd never been able to afford, and never thought I would. Finally, almost like I was sleep talking, like I couldn't even control myself, I just said it aloud. "Fifty dollars."

I hadn't even known Ira was awake, but he was. "Fifty dollars ain't nothing," he said.

"Papa didn't make fifty dollars in three months working for the WPA," I said. "Not a whole summer day, fifteen hours."

"Fifty dollars won't buy you an air-cooled Franklin," Ira said. "It might not even buy you a ride in one."

"It's a start, though," I said.

"It's a start," he agreed. "All we got to do now is stick with it."

"Through thick or thin," I said.

And I knew that was what he wanted me to say, because then he turned over, and I could hear him start snoring within a minute or two. Not me, though. I laid awake for a long time thinking about that. It was the first fifty-dollar bill I'd ever seen.

Through thick or thin. And we didn't know nothing about the thin times then, but they sure enough came along.

CHAPTER 11

CHATTANOOGA

Well, the next thing you know, Ira got married. Nobody saw it coming, but there he was, hitched to this local gal by the name of Annie Lou Roberts, and they had a little girl, Gail, together. That meant Ira had to find some way to support his family besides working for Papa. So he and his wife moved to Rome, Georgia, and he got a job pushing a Good Humor ice cream cart for a short time.

One reason why he left Sand Mountain and married, I guess, was that he'd had enough of being treated like a slave by Papa, just like our sisters did. But there was another reason, too. There was all kinds of rumors going around about women who'd come up pregnant after spending some time with him. Of course, Ira always denied he was the father of any of 'em, but I never quite believed him. Even back then, Ira never had any problem convincing the ladies to do pretty much whatever he wanted. And he always had his eye on at least two.

Of course, it turned out that pushing an ice cream cart wasn't enough for Ira to pay the bills, so it wasn't too long before he lit out for Chattanooga, Tennessee, where he got a job for the Peerless Woolen Mills. But he still came back down to the farm on the weekends and we kept playing every little event we could find.

And then one weekend he rolled onto the farm, just busting with some news he'd heard. One of the Chattanooga radio stations was holding an amateur contest, and Ira was sure we could win. Even though Papa didn't think much of the idea, it didn't cost nobody nothing, so he let me go.

The way the contest worked was that each act would play three different Saturday nights, and if one of the acts could win all three events, they'd get a fifteen-minute radio show. Now, it wasn't much of a show. It aired at four thirty in the morning on a tiny 250-watt radio station, WDEF. But still, it'd be our very own, and it seemed like the biggest thing in the world to us.

The first night of the contest, we did a silly little song called "There's a Hole in the Bottom of the Sea," and, sure enough, we won. The following Saturday night, we did a song our Mama had taught us that wasn't silly at all called "The Knoxville Girl." And we won again. The third night we switched back to "There's a Hole in the Bottom of the Sea." And we won for the third time.

We knew we were pretty good, but that was the first chance we'd really had the chance to show it off and let everybody see what we could do. And we knew we couldn't lose. Getting our own radio show was the real beginning. Everybody with a radio could hear us if they'd just tune in. We started working on Papa immediately, and somehow Ira talked him into allowing me to come to Chattanooga, where I got a job at the cotton mill.

It was rough work. There was this big hopper where they

put the wool, and the machine would turn it into threads and then wind 'em up on a roller. When the roller got about twelve or fourteen inches thick, we'd cut the strings, pull it off, and replace it with an empty one. Each of us had four of those machines we had to keep up with, and I guarantee you enough bosses were around that we couldn't relax for more than forty-five seconds before one of them was down there wanting to know what was wrong. They called those mills sweatshops even back then.

It didn't hurt us, but it convinced us that working in a woolen mill wasn't what we wanted to do for the rest of our lives. And maybe it helped us understand that working for Papa wasn't really any worse than working for anybody else. If you're killing yourself to make somebody else money, there ain't no future in it. Getting up in the morning and punching that card to work eight and a half hours before you could punch it again and leave wasn't a whole lot different from Papa's slavery.

It was exhausting, especially with the radio show. And knowing that we needed all the practice we could get, we were still working as many free shows as we could. You could always find a nursing home or a veterans' hospital you could play in the afternoon, and it's good for you, the practice.

The radio station was tiny. It was the smallest in Chattanooga, and it didn't have a recording room. There was just a little four-by-four closet with a microphone hanging from the ceiling. Maybe twenty-five or thirty years later, most of the stations had more room because they got a lot of live bluegrass and country bands, but in those days there was barely room for the two of us and the announcer, who would stay put in his little cubby in case there was a car wreck or something that folks would want to know about right away.

Anyway, we did a few radio programs, and then Ira thought to ask for mail, to see if anybody had written to us. And, sure enough, we had a letter from Jasper, Tennessee, about forty miles out of Chattanooga toward Nashville. They wanted us to come down and play for the PTA.

We rolled into Jasper with a little old Bogen sound system, one microphone, a guitar, and a mandolin. They'd set us up upstairs of the courthouse, in the courtroom, and it was packed with people. So we walked right in and played the show. The deal was that the PTA would get thirty percent of what came in at the door, and we'd get seventy. And our part of the show that night came to a hundred dollars apiece.

"A hundred dollars this time," Ira said on the drive back to the place we were sharing in Chattanooga. It was only our second paying gig, and it seemed like fate was on our side as we were holding that money. Only our second show and we'd already doubled our rate. If you could make this kind of money with an early morning show on the smallest station in Chattanooga, we just knew this was our golden ladder and it was gonna take us straight up.

"A hundred dollars apiece," I corrected him. It was Ira's car, a used one, but I was driving. Even back then, he liked to have a couple beers after we played a show, and I didn't like to ride with anybody who wasn't dead sober.

"I'll bet we'll get more letters, too," Ira said.

"We've probably already got more," I said.

"We're sticking with this. Thick or thin." That was something he said all the time back then. It was as if he wanted to make sure that I wasn't gonna jump ship or anything.

That was the thing about Ira, as much as he was convinced the music was all his doing, he always seemed scared that I'd give up on it. He could be so cocky and reckless you couldn't believe some of the things he'd do, and yet need your approval so much it'd just eat him up. He would do everything he could to show the world he didn't need anybody, but those of us who knew him knew that underneath all that bullshit, he was probably the most insecure man who ever walked the planet.

He needn't have worried. Shit, we were big shots now. We called ourselves the Radio Twins, and before long, we had more mail than we could handle. We didn't have no booking agency or anything, so I wrote all the folks back by myself and we worked every show we could. Our life got even busier. Up at three, drink coffee, off to the radio show, and then back for a quick breakfast and a full day at the mill. Then off to a show, which we wouldn't get back from until one or two in the morning.

We didn't stay on that little radio show for long, though. Eventually, we moved over to the more powerful WDOD and joined up with a group. We had a comedian and two musicians. One of them was a boy who could sing a song if you needed him to, and the other played upright bass. We did pretty well with those boys, and gave ourselves the name Foggy Mountain Boys.

The funny thing was, Lester Flatt and Earl Scruggs came up with the same name later, and when they broke up, they had a lawsuit going about who owned the rights to it. Lester thought it should be Lester Flatt and the Foggy Mountain Boys, and Earl thought it should be Earl Scruggs and the Foggy Mountain Boys. Well, one night, I ran into Lester backstage at a show we were playing together, and I said, "Lester, what in the hell are you boys doing suing each other?"

"Well," Lester said, "Earl claims the name belongs to him because he wrote the 'Foggy Mountain Breakdown.' And I say that I came up with the name before he even wrote that song."

"Shit," I said, "it don't belong to either damn one of you."

He kind of looked at me funny. "What do you mean? Sure it does."

"No, it doesn't," I said. And I showed him an eight-by-ten

picture of me, Ira, and the two other guys, and plainly written over it all was the Foggy Mountain Boys.

They never did settle the lawsuit. I think Earl called his band The Earl Scruggs Review, and Lester just used Lester Flatt. They were acting like children. Suing each other over a name. There are too many names out there to sue somebody over one. Which is something I learned real well later on.

CHAPTER 12

BUCK DANCING

Even as hard as we were working, we weren't making near enough money to live on, so we had to dig for ways to come up with cash any way we could. One of those was to sing in pool joints. They didn't have jukeboxes in those days. The only music they had was whatever a band could provide. Now you can't make a living like that, but back then there was nothing but the clicking of the cue ball to liven up a pool hall.

I'll never forget this one pool hall. It was run by this crook who'd pay us to clear beer bottles off the tables in between songs. Only instead of throwing the beer bottles away, he'd have us take all the half-full beers over to this special cooler, where he would fill them up with other half-full beers and twist a new cap on them. Then when some guy got tipsy enough where he couldn't tell one beer from another, this

Inside the pool hall

guy would sell him one of the old beers. Hell, he'd fill up more than a hundred and fifty bottles of beer a night that way. You wouldn't believe how many half-full beers people will walk off and leave. We'd clear tables like that for an hour, and then get up and play some music.

Then we started working with this friend of ours. His name was Jimmy, and he was a buck dancing fool. Ira would pick a fast tune on the mandolin and I'd give him a little guitar accompaniment, and Jimmy would do his thing until he was wore out. Then Ira and I would sing a song while he was catching his breath. After we got done, Jimmy would dance around with his hat. As long as the hat came back with money in it, we'd sing another song. And when it came back empty, we'd move on to another joint.

Bless his heart, Jimmy was a great guy, a gentle guy, but

he got in a fight wherever he went. Seemed like every night somebody would call him a sissy. He was everything but a sissy, but for some reason he liked to wear his hat turned down a little in the front, and some people thought that made him look like one.

I remember there was this restaurant, the Crystal, right on Main Street in Chattanooga. We used to go in for what we called gut bombs, a burger and a small cola, which you could get cheaper than any other meal in town. Well, one time we was in there, and Jimmy was sitting down at the bar with us, drinking coffee with his burger, and some guy way back at the other end of the bar spotted him, got the waiter, ordered a glass of milk, and said, "Take it down there to that guy with the little hat on, I'll pay for it."

So the waiter took the milk and set it in front of Jimmy, and Jimmy looked around to see if he could find out who did it. Sure enough, he spotted the guy down yonder, and the guy made a gesture at him, like, drink up. We knew right then that it was only a matter of time before Jimmy hit him. The guy didn't know it, but we did.

Jimmy'd act like a pussy. He'd act as if you couldn't agitate him into a fight. But when he got you in the right place, he was like a stroke of lightning. He was so quick your ass was out cold before you ever knew the fight had started. And that's what happened. He waited, didn't drink none of the milk, and when he was done with his burger, he got up and started out, stopping at the counter to pay for his food. Then, when he passed the guy who'd ordered him the milk, he turned around and winked at him.

That pissed the guy off for sure. He came running out of the restaurant, looking for a fight. But as soon as he hit the sidewalk, Jimmy just cold-cocked him. Knocked him out completely.

That was the kind of guy Jimmy was. He didn't take no

guff from nobody. He was a fightin' dude, and he was a fair fighter. He wouldn't use no knucks or no knives, he'd just outfight you with his bare fists. He didn't care who it was, neither. He'd fight a cop just as soon as anybody else. Five cops caught him one night and were beating him, and he managed to get away and almost outrun all five of them. And, then, when they did catch up to him, he laid three of them out on the cement.

He was a good friend of ours, a phenomenal man, and he introduced us to what we called the carnival life, playing on the street. We made pretty good money together, too. Sometimes as much as ten or fifteen dollars a night. In Chattanooga down on the Georgia line, where Tennessee lies on one side and Georgia on the other, there was a walkway where people had to come through to get to the main street. We'd get in the walkway, set up, and start picking and singing right there, and the money would roll in.

People out walking would stop to listen, and people in the buildings would open their windows and hang their heads out. The next thing you'd know, the whole alley'd be totally clogged.

And, of course, somebody would report it to the cops and they'd come run us off. But twenty minutes later, we'd be right back in there again. We drove them cops wild.

CHAPTER 13

WELCOME
TO THE
ARMY

Unfortunately, our high times in Chattanooga didn't last long. We got picked off by the Army. The first to go was Ira, drafted. He wasn't gone long, though. If you had the displeasure of being in the military back in the middle part of the twentieth century, you'll know they always had this eight-foot square hole they wanted you to swing over on a rope to prove something or another. That was one of the exercises in basic training. You'd run as fast as you could go, and when you come to the edge of this hole, you'd jump and catch the rope and your momentum would swing you to the other side, and that's where you were supposed to turn loose of it. I can't imagine anything more stupid, but everybody had to do it.

Well, my brother, he was never coordinated at all, and when he hit that other side, he didn't turn loose of the rope in time. And when the rope slipped out of his hand, he fell to the bottom of that eight-foot hole. Worse, there was this unconcerned sergeant who was supposed to be watching, and he didn't notice that Ira didn't make it, so he sent the next man. And the next man also couldn't make the edge, and he fell right in the middle of my brother's back.

It messed Ira up good. They call it spondylosis. He was never up to par after that when it come to lifting or driving or whatever. But the worst thing was that when the Army discharged him, they said they'd only let him go if he signed a piece of paper saying he'd only been in for eighty-nine days, since they knew you had to be in for ninety days to get the GI Bill. They knew exactly what they were doing, but he was so glad to get out he would have took it at fifty days. So he didn't get nothing from the Army, even with an injury that plagued him the rest of his life.

After he got drafted I moved back down on the farm with Mama and Papa, and I sure was excited to see him when he walked in the door. I didn't think I could take much more of Papa's farmwork. But when Ira and I tried to get back in the music business, we didn't have no luck. And, even worse, I couldn't get a day job. I was just eighteen years old, and every time I applied for a job, they told me, "Hey, the draft will have you before we can even get you trained."

I heard that so many times that I just woke up one morning and said, "There's only one way to cure this." So I went down to the recruiter and joined up with the Air Force.

They put us on a train like cattle and shipped us to Fort Polk, Louisiana. That's where everybody picked up the clothes they were issued. Then they put us on another train to Lowry Air Force Base in Denver, where they sent me to mechanic's school. It's funny that you'd join the Air Force and they'd send you to mechanic's school, but they did.

I spent the whole time learning how to take apart and put together cars. They'd spread a transmission apart in pieces over the floor, and give you an hour to put it together so it'd work. The same thing with an engine. If you wanted to pass

In the Army

the class, you had to be able to take one apart and put it together, piece by piece, with a stopwatch going. And then be able to crank it up to prove it worked.

I got pretty good at it, but I had no interest, not even a little bit, in following it as a trade. Not because it was a dirty job or anything like that, just because I was hooked on music and there was nothing else I wanted to do. Once music gets into your blood, if anybody tries to get you to do anything else, you're constantly trying to figure out how to get back to it. That and you can't get on the Opry by rebuilding engines.

Knowing a little about cars used to help me out some when

we were on the road, though. At least until they computerized everything. The shade tree mechanic today don't stand a pig's chance. If you raise the hood and throw a marble in there, the chances are pretty good it won't even touch the ground. The compartments are so crowded, you can't see through them, and even if the most minor thing in the engine goes bad, you have to work four hours just so you can get to it.

I only stayed in the Air Force fourteen months. When I started they would take a little of my money from each check and put some of their money with it, and send it home to Mama and Papa. But after fourteen months, they decided to cut out that program, so they told us that if we were really needed at home, we could get out early. Well, I'd had all I needed of the Air Force, I can tell you that, so I went up to headquarters and got that discharge.

I found Ira in Knoxville, singing bass with Charlie Monroe and the Kentucky Pardners. The best tenor in the world singing bass, if you can imagine that. He even recorded a few songs with them in Chicago. But as soon as I showed up, he quit and we got back together again.

It was about this time that we started using the Louvin name instead of Loudermilk. People couldn't pronounce Loudermilk, let alone spell it, and some just laughed out loud when they heard it. We'd tried working for a while as the Sand Mountain Playboys, but that never did suit us, so we took the first three letters of our name, added "vin" to them, and became the Louvin Brothers. I have no idea where it came from, but that's what we did.

I know that at times Papa was hurt that we'd changed our names. Especially later, after we got popular. When he'd be out peddling vegetables or sorghum in Chattanooga, there was this little restaurant where he'd stop to get a bite to eat, and before he got his food, he liked to get up and take a look at the jukebox to see how many records we had on there. If he saw two or three of his favorites, he'd drop the coins in and play them. Then, when the waitress would bring his food over, he'd say to her, as proud as could be, "Those are my boys."

She would always say the same thing. "Oh, I know what you mean, sir. They're our boys, too."

I know that hurt him. He had no way of proving that the two Louvin Brothers singing really were his children. But he took it pretty well. And he made up for it when we stopped by the house. It was just like when we were kids and company would show up, invited or uninvited. The first thing Papa would say when somebody came in the living room and got seated was, "You boys get your instruments and sing the good people a couple of songs."

It got worse the more people heard us on the radio. Seemed like every time we stopped by the house there was a dozen people waiting for us. It aggravated Ira so much that he almost quit going by the house altogether.

I still don't know how Papa did it. I'd call them up at maybe eight o'clock in the morning and tell Mama, "We was in Georgia last night, and we're on the way home. We thought we might stop by for a bit."

"What time will you be here, son?" she'd ask.

"I can't say for sure because you can't judge the traffic," I'd say. "But we certainly oughta be there by an hour or so after dinner."

Most people didn't have phones on Sand Mountain at that time, but sure enough there'd be twenty people sitting in the living room when we walked in, some of whom we'd never even seen. The only thing I can figure is that Papa must have sent my sisters running house to house in every direction.

One time Ira managed to get Papa outside and ask him, "What are all these people doing here, Papa?

"What do you mean, what are they doing here?" Papa asked right back.

"I don't know a single one of them. Ain't never seen one of them before in my life."

"Well, they're my neighbors and it's my house," Papa said. "You don't have to know them. I do."

"All I'm saying is that we'd like to be able to stop by and see the family without doing a damn show," Ira said.

"I didn't ask you what you liked," Papa said. "Now get in there and do your thing."

Ira didn't ask no more questions after that. You couldn't tell Papa no, and you couldn't reason with him. So Ira just swallowed down what he was thinking and did the shows. For my part, I didn't mind so much, but every time we drove away from the house you could have choked to death on Ira's anger, the air was so thick with it. And I'd know better than to say a word.

CHAPTER 14

THE FORTUNE-TELLER

After I got back from Denver and Ira quit with Charlie Monroe and the Kentucky Pardners in Knoxville, we teamed up with another pair of brothers, Hack and Clyde Johnson, and got a regular gospel show on WNOX. Even though it aired at five thirty in the morning, the mail started pouring in just like before, asking us to play. Sometimes we'd tour with Hack and Clyde, and sometimes we'd do our own shows as the Louvin Brothers.

It was at one of those shows that one of the strangest things of our career happened.

We were playing a fair in Danville, Virginia, and after we got done, Ira and I took a walk around, enjoying the night air and the lights, taking a gander at the games and the girls. And then Ira spotted a fortune-teller's tent.

"Let's go in there and see what she has to say," Ira said.

"I ain't got no need to go in there," I said. "I don't put no stock in that shit."

"Oh Lord," Ira said. "Here comes the lecture."

He knew me pretty well, I guess, because I was sure enough getting ready to lecture him. You can weather any storm if you believe that it's gonna be better on down the road. I've adopted that theory in my life, and I know it's better than trusting in carnival hucksters. You gotta just do your thing and trust in the Lord. "Good things and bad things are gonna happen in everybody's life," I said. "That's what the Good Book says. And it says, 'It will come to pass.' "

"I know the Good Book better than you do," Ira said in an irritated voice. "I'm going in. I don't care what you do."

"You ain't gotta get sulky about it," I said, and we ducked inside the tent. It was full of all the usual fortune-teller junk. A crystal ball, incense, the whole bit. But there was no discounting what she told us. That we were gonna meet a new face. A big, tall man, wearing a large Stetson hat and a suit. And he was gonna be good for us, if we did what he asked.

Well, we laughed it off at first. We figured Knoxville was where we were really gonna get our career rolling. It wasn't the kind of town where you might get a record contract, we knew that. It also wasn't the kind of place where you might get somebody to notice you and want to be your booker. But they called it the training ground for the Grand Ole Opry. The word was that once you'd been a trainee of Knoxville for a year or so, you had a chance to be on the Opry, and, of course, that was all we ever wanted.

At first it was working, too. We were playing shows regular, and even bought a new car. It wasn't an air-cooled Franklin limousine, but it was a nice little Ambassador Nash, with an inline six-cylinder in it. It was our first road car, a good mountain car that ran like a top in the hills.

It was a little on the small side, I'll admit. Once we loaded it up with all the equipment and then Ira, Clyde, Hack, and me piled in, you barely had room to breathe. We had to push in the doghouse bass last, with one side of the body on the shoulder of the man directly behind the driver, the other side on the shoulder of the man behind the passenger, and the neck running up through the seats where they separated. Then you'd just hope to God you didn't run into anything or have to stop real quick, because if you did, that bass fiddle'd fly through the windshield like it wasn't even there.

We lost a few of 'em that way. It got so we'd tie them on top of the vehicle, but that wasn't a whole lot better. You'd be going down the road at sixty-five or seventy miles an hour, one of those ropes would break, and you'd hear this mild thump before you looked in the mirror and saw it tumbling down the road behind you. You'd know right then that you was gonna borrow a bass fiddle from somebody that night.

The shows around Knoxville dried up pretty quick, though. You can only play so many spots within driving distance of where you're located before you get played out, especially if you don't have any records for sale. We were broke again, and it was me, Ira, and his wife, Annie Lou, all living together in a one-room apartment in this great big old house. Everything was in that one room. Bathroom, kitchen, bed, and a big couch, which is where I slept. Lucky for me, their baby Gail didn't cry much, not even enough to wake me up. It was starting to get plain discouraging, and neither Ira nor I had any idea what our next move should be.

Then it happened just like that fortune-teller had said it would. One morning, Ira and I were eating breakfast at this little restaurant across from WNOX. They'd sell you cornflakes cheaper than you could get any other breakfast in town, so Ira and I ate a bowl there every morning after our radio show.

All of a sudden this yacht of a car pulled up out front, parked right in a no parking zone, and this big, strapping man, probably six foot four, kicked out from behind the wheel, adjusting his belt. He had a face like the moon, and you could tell that when he threw a smile across it, it'd eclipse everything else in sight. And he was wearing a large Stetson hat.

Ira and I looked at each other, but we didn't say nothing. There was all kinds of that type in Knoxville, and we didn't figure there could be any way that he was there to see us, no matter what any fortune-teller had said. But he opened the door to the restaurant, stood in the doorway blocking out most of it, and, after spotting us, walked straight over to our table. "Hello boys," he said, sliding right in across from us. "What are you eating?"

"Cornflakes," I said.

"Well, that won't do," he said. "I can't have the world's greatest duet eating goddamn cornflakes." By then, the waitress had come over to see what he wanted. "Country ham and eggs," he told her. "And an order for each of them, too."

When she left, he sat back in his chair and eyed us. He had this big diamond ring that you could tell we was supposed to be impressed with. We found out later that he'd borrowed it. Along with the suit, and the car, too. He was really putting on the dog. "Gentleman," he said. "My name's Smilin' Eddie Hill, and I'm here to offer you the job of a lifetime."

"What's the job?" Ira asked.

"It's like this," Eddie said, "I've got a show all sold to a radio station in Memphis. They're ready to buy it right now. The hitch is that I've promised them the world's best band and the world's best duet. I've got the world's best band, but I still need that duet, and that's where y'all come in."

Well, it's hard to argue with a job when you're eating cornflakes. So we agreed to join up with him right there. It only seemed fair, anyhow, seeing as how hard he'd worked to impress us. Harder than he had to, really. A decent meal alone would have done it.

That wasn't Eddie's way, though. He was a born showman, and half carnival huckster, himself. One story he liked to tell was about when he was a teenager, starting out like us, and he was playing a little country fair in Polk County, Tennessee. He was just about to get up onstage to start playing, when this cop put his hand on his arm.

"What do you think you're doing, germ?" Eddie said, looking down at him. Eddie wasn't nearly above laying out a cop if he was given a reason. And as big as he was, he didn't have much trouble doing so, even as a teenager.

"Is your name Eddie Hill?" the cop asked.

"That's right. And I'm just about to get up on this stage and play my set."

"Not with that guitar you ain't," the cop said. "You've missed payments on it and I'm here to repossess it."

"Aw, c'mon," Eddie said. "We're just about to play a show here. How's about you let us do our thing, and whatever we make we'll turn over toward the payments?"

The cop waffled. He really wanted to take the guitar, especially after the way Eddie'd introduced himself. "It don't make any sense in the world to take this guitar without letting me see if I can get any money out of it," Eddie continued.

"All right," the cop finally agreed. "But don't try stepping past me without handing over the payments or the guitar."

"You got it," Eddie said, and hopped up on the stage. And, sure enough, he made enough money that night to pay the guitar off in full. Which he tossed at the cop's feet on his way past him.

He'd started in the music business playing bass on the Midday Merry-Go-Round on WNOX, led up by Johnnie Wright and Jack Anglin, who played under the name Johnnie & Jack. They were a pretty good country duet back in the day. Eddie's big break came when Jack Anglin got drafted, and Johnnie picked him as his replacement. Of course, Eddie being Eddie, he didn't stay with them long. He wanted his own show, and that was why he was pitching us.

We didn't waste any time, either. The next day, we shipped

Ira's wife and daughter back to her people until Ira could send for her, and he and I drove down to Memphis and found a place to stay. It was a joint called the Blackwell Hotel, and both of us could bunk in one room for seven dollars a week each. Of course, Eddie was only paying us twenty, but we also found a restaurant downtown where we could eat two meals a day for another seven a week, and that left us six dollars for toothpaste and cigarettes. We didn't have a worry in the world.

CHAPTER 15

WE CAME
TO
HEAR YOU
SING

Eddie made us earn our twenty dollars a week. He had us working three shows a day on WMPS. There was an early morning show at five thirty, where Ira and I played a country song and a hymn. Then there was the High Noon Roundup, where we played with the whole Eddie Hill band, including Paul Buskirk on mandolin and guitar, Tony Cianciola on accordion, and a steel guitar, bass, and piano. It may not have been the best band in the world, but it was one of 'em. They could play everything from swing to string band. And lastly, we had an afternoon show called the Lonesome Valley Trio, just Eddie and us playing gospel songs.

Even though we were low paid, that job with Smilin' Eddie Hill was the best thing that ever happened to the Louvin Brothers. Just doing those little old-timey songs we knew, some of 'em gospel, some of 'em old folk songs, we received ten thousand pieces of mail a week. Penny postcards, letters, everything. If we ever had a hot spot going for us, it was Memphis. We just couldn't do any wrong there.

We drove everywhere. We worked campgrounds, fairs, everywhere we could. We'd drive all the way up into Pennsylvania or New York or Maryland for a show. We didn't have busses and we didn't take planes. By the time you could fly up to Philadelphia and have somebody pick you up and drive up to Sunset Park or New River Ranch, it took just as long as driving, anyway. I had my little Studebaker, which I was pretty proud of, and Eddie usually rode separately in a Cadillac limo driven by his accordion player, Tony.

We missed out on a lot of sleep, but that was part of the business. Besides, they had pills for it. Some of the boys back then, they took them even if they never got close to the steering wheel, just to get high, but I used 'em to drive. I had to. Ira couldn't hardly drive at all because of his back and, sometimes, the beer.

I used to be able to get them that were called Old Yellers, and one of them would carry me five hundred miles to do a show and five hundred miles back without sleep. Other people would take one starting out and then two more to make it there, and then three to get back home, but I never could take that many. My body's too timid. I couldn't handle 'em all.

We were always racing the clock, pulling up just as the show was about to start. We'd pile out of the cars, and the first thing I'd say to the show's organizer was, "You got a creek around here?"

"Right down there," they'd say, and point me at it.

So I'd step down to the creek, and it'd be running just as clear and cold as could be, and I'd pour that water up on my face, then take my handkerchief and dry off, and say, "All right, let's go."

So far, it hasn't killed me. But some artists just won't do it.

Most of today's artists, I'd say about ninety percent of them, they get on their bus in Nashville, pull off their clothes, get in the bunk, and lay down the whole way. They just go to bed. They got an air conditioner and a television in their bunk, and they can pretty much do whatever they want. They ride all night long, and the next day when they get to Albuquerque or wherever, they pull into the motel and the first words out of their mouth is, "Where's my room?" They slept all the way, ten hours or twelve, and that's the first words out of their mouth.

And, of course, they stay in their room until the last second before the show. Then they get out, play the concert, and as soon as it's done, they're back in the bus ready to go home. That's the way they want it, no hassle. You can ask them to meet the fans or do an autograph session, but they won't bother unless it's scheduled. They'll tell you, "We don't want no hassle. We didn't make this trip to do an autograph session, we're just working."

Back in our day, we never had the luxury of not wanting to be hassled. I remember once we did a show at this schoolhouse in a little town in eastern Kentucky. You had to park down the road and cross a swinging bridge to get to it. I remember it real well, because they had a no talking rule for the audience. If anybody had even tried to blow their nose, I have the feeling they might have been killed by those big Kentucky boys. I've never played to an audience that was completely silent like that. It was a little spooky.

Anyway, after we finished our show, a pretty nice show without any distractions, we were walking back toward that swinging bridge when we ran face to face with about eight Kentucky boys. Every one of them was bigger than Eddie, and they'd just got out of the mine. Still had the coal dust on their face and everything.

"Oh, shit, the show's not over, is it?" one of them asked.

"It sure is," Eddie said. "We were just heading out."

"Well," the miner said, "we really wanted to hear you sing."

"That's right," another one said, "we got here as early as we could, and we'd really love to hear a few songs."

You could just tell by the tone of their voice that they weren't really asking us. That what they meant was that if we wanted to leave with our instruments whole, well, we'd better get them out and play a few songs. So we did. Even Eddie, who I don't think I'd ever seen take orders from anybody, wasn't about to tell these boys no. We sure as hell weren't about to tell them we didn't want to be hassled. We asked them what they wanted to hear, and we did a half dozen songs right out in the front yard.

"Thank you," the first miner said, and he shook Eddie's hand, and then Ira's, and then mine, and all the way down the line. And each of them followed along, shaking each of our hands in turn. "Would you like us to carry your instruments to the car?" one of them asked.

"That's all right," Eddie said. "We can carry them."

"How about money?" the miner said. "Can we pay you something?"

"No need," Eddie said, shaking his head. "Happy to do it."

They were as nice as can be, but if we'd said no to playing those songs, I'm not sure we would have made it out of there in one piece. And I know our instruments wouldn't have.

CHAPTER 16

SODA CRACKERS

You never quite know what you're gonna run into on the road. One of the strangest and greatest surprises of my life came just after we started up with Eddie. We were booked at a show in Dyess, Arkansas, and we arrived about thirty or forty minutes late. The school auditorium had already filled up with people, and since it was my job to sell the tickets, I had to be the asshole that went in and told all of them that were already sitting inside waiting for the music, "I'm sorry, folks, but we're running a few minutes late. I'm gonna have to ask you to get up and go out and come in again, so's I can sell you tickets."

That didn't set well with anybody, I'm sure. But they got up and went out, and I sold them all tickets as they filed back in. When I got done, and the building was just about full, I noticed this kid standing out there in overalls. Probably fourteen years old with no shirt, no hat, and no shoes. Just overalls and a tan that you would not believe a human could have.

You could tell he was naturally dark skinned, but it was late in the fall, right toward the end of the cotton-picking season, and he'd obviously gone through the whole summer dressed just as I saw him.

Well, we'd been driving for a long time and it had taken me some time to get all the tickets sold, so I was just about to piss on myself. "Son, do y'all have restrooms?" I asked him.

"Sure thing, mister," he said, and led me out to the out-house.

I went in and took a leak, and when I came out, I found that he was still sitting there, waiting on me. Like I said, I'd been driving hard all day, and I hadn't been able to stop for food or anything, but I remembered I had a package of saltine crackers in my pocket. I ripped the package open and ate a cracker while we walked back up to the schoolhouse.

"Mister, why are you eating those crackers?" the kid asked.

"To keep from starving to death," I answered. I realize now it was a smart-ass answer, but I didn't mean it to be at the time.

He didn't say nothing to that, and when we got back to the schoolhouse, he stood around out front, and I could tell he didn't have no money to come inside. So I said, "I'll tell you what, son, you just come on in and sit right there on that bench by the door."

He got uncomfortable and shifted around in his overalls. He didn't like the idea of taking advantage of anything he hadn't paid for. "I'm waiting on friends," he said. "If I'm not out here, they won't know how to find me."

"That's all right," I said. "The door's wide open, and when they get here, they'll see you sitting there. You can bring them in with you on that bench."

"I don't have no money," he admitted.

"I didn't say nothing about money, did I?" I said. "Get on in here. That whole bench is for you and your friends."

"All right," he said, reluctantly. "All right. Thank you, mister."

"Call me Charlie," I said.

I forgot about him as the show started. And when we got done, I didn't see him as we piled into our cars, waved good-bye, and left. It wasn't until years later that I realized who that boy was, and only when he told me.

It was Johnny Cash. He'd snuck down to see the show, just the way Ira and I had seen Roy Acuff not so long ago, by standing outside the school and listening with all the other folks who didn't have no money.

And I heard that for years afterward, whenever John was getting ready to start singing, he would always eat two soda crackers before he went onstage. He thought there was something about those soda crackers that had to do with the way I sounded. Of course, it's probably the worst thing you could do, to put crackers on your throat when you're about to sing, but I guess it worked for him.

Much later, he told me how I'd gotten him in trouble another time without knowing it, too. He had this three-dollar-a-day job carrying water for a dredging crew on the Tyronza River, and when the crew went back to work after lunch, John would sneak into this man's pickup truck and turn on the radio to listen to our Lonesome Valley Trio gospel show out of Memphis. After the show, John would hop out of that truck, switch it off, and run like crazy down to the crew to bring 'em water, because, of course, he'd be late with it by then.

Well, one day he was in a rush and he didn't turn the ignition off when the program was over. And that afternoon when the work was finished, that man went to his pickup and tried to fire up the engine, but the battery was dead. When that old boy found that the radio had been left on, it didn't take much to connect the dots to that water boy who was late every day after lunch. So not only did I almost cost John his voice, I got him fired from one of his first jobs.

I wasn't too far from being a kid myself when we met that first time. But when we met up again after he started recording and performing, we became fast friends. And we never stopped being friends, right up to when he passed away.

Johnny Cash and the Louvin Brothers

CHAPTER 17

ANNIE LOU
AND
BETTY

Ira and Annie Lou weren't even trying to get along anymore. They did nothing but fight. A big part of the problem was that, just like our sisters, Ira married way too young. He wasn't but seventeen when they got hitched, and Gail was born before his eighteenth birthday. Their marriage was like a candle in a winter window. On fire today and turned to ice tomorrow. It got so they couldn't even be in the same room together, and finally, Annie Lou took Gail and moved back to Sand Mountain.

Once she'd left town, Ira got a lawyer right away, and the lawyer told him, "Get a place to live, a nice apartment, and then put a notice for three weeks in a row in the local paper. Tell her to come on home, and give the address. If she doesn't come out to live with you by the end of three days, we'll charge her with desertion."

So that's what Ira did, and Annie Lou didn't get a red cent out of him. It was a trick, of course. Naturally, she wouldn't get a Memphis paper down in Alabama. But it was legal back then, though I kindly hope it's not anymore.

It was about that time that I first saw Betty Harrison. It was after one of our Lonesome Valley Trio shows. Eddie, Ira, and I walked out of the WMPS studios and over to the Walgreens across the street to get some food, and there she was, working behind the lunch counter. She was a broad-faced beauty, with curly black hair and eyes that lit up all over the place whenever she smiled. And she smiled all the time, spinning around to take an empty cup of coffee, delivering a plate of food. I felt my chest swell up, and just prayed to God that Ira didn't take an interest in her. I never had a chance with any woman Ira got his eye on.

Betty Harrison, age 17

We sat down at the lunch counter, propping our instruments up by the stools. We were always a little crazy after a session, pulling on each other's arms and cracking jokes, and that's what Ira and Eddie were doing. I couldn't stop staring at her, though. "Do y'all work for the radio?" she asked, setting out water for us.

"Ma'am," Eddie said, "you are looking at the finest duet in all the world." He clapped Ira and me on our shoulders when he said it, and continued. "And I'm Smilin' Eddie Hill, the greatest master of ceremonies this town has ever known."

"Well, finest duet in the world and Mr. Smilin' Eddie Hill," she said. "What can I get you to eat?"

Eddie reached into his pocket as if to pull out a great roll of bills, but only came up with coins. It'd been a little too long since we'd been on the road. But he slapped it down on the counter and said, "We'll have all the food that thirty-seven cents can buy."

Lord, she laughed. "I'll tell you what," she said, leaning on the counter. "I can't let the finest duet and greatest master of ceremonies in the world go hungry. Why don't each of you order up something, and I'll see what I can do."

It went that way from then on out. All of us would go in together, and she'd feed us for free if we didn't have no money. And then it was just Ira and me going in there. And then it was just me. And she and I'd sit and talk for hours on end.

There's an old saying that says that the way to get to a man's heart is through his stomach. That's not the only reason I fell in love with her, of course, but when you're real hungry it doesn't hurt. And there ain't nothing a picker and a grinner likes more than a free meal.

She had more spirit than any six girls I'd ever known. She had a mischievous side that couldn't be beat, but she was also a hard-working gal. She'd started working at Walgreens when she was only fourteen years old. She'd go to school, work at Walgreens until one o'clock in the night, and then get up in the morning to do the dishes her sister saved for her, eat a bowl of oatmeal, and walk the two miles back to school again.

After sitting there talking to her over the lunch counter for weeks, I finally screwed up the courage to ask her if I could stop by her house to visit her sometime. She said yes, but I'm still not entirely sure she knew I was courting her even then. She was a real naïve girl when I met her. I don't believe she'd ever really noticed any boys before me. She grew up in a house with eight brothers and sisters, and about the only time she noticed a boy was when one said something to her that she didn't like. Then she and all her brothers and sisters would gang up and make him eat dirt.

Most people would probably say it wasn't the courtship she deserved. I'd sit with her at her house when I was in town, and I'd usually stay all day, but we never really dated. We didn't go out to movies or dinner or anything like that very much. Part of the reason was that I was a little scared of spooking her by moving too fast, but the other was that I never had no money. I mean, I was the only guy she ever went with if she was going anywhere, but we never went much of anywhere. We just sat and enjoyed each other's company. Which, if you think about it, is probably the best kind of courting, anyway.

CHAPTER 18

SMILIN' EDDIE HILL, ARRESTED

On the road, even serious guys get a little funny. And Eddie, he was worse than most. To give you an example of his sense of humor, this one night he was driving his Continental convertible back from a show, and Ira and I were in the car with him, along with Paul Buskirk. Eddie actually had three cars. The two Cadillac limos, what we usually drove, and then the Continental, which he'd take if he had a girl wherever we were doing the show date. That way he didn't have to come and go with nobody.

Ira was up front with Eddie, and I was riding in the backseat with Paul, who was fast asleep. We came to a place where the road turned alongside some railroad tracks, taking us right up next to them, and just as we was fixing to make that right turn next to the tracks, a train blew its whistle. So Eddie took advantage of it and slammed on the brakes, playing like he was about to be hit.

It scared Paul so bad he almost shit his britches. He woke

up flailing and screaming, just terrified that Eddie'd run out in front of a train. Oh, Lord, we laughed. And, of course, it pissed Paul off, big time. He grumbled and complained about halfway back to Memphis, but finally he went back to sleep.

Well, what we usually did when we went out on the road was to park all of our cars down by the river, and then pile into one of Eddie's cars, and he'd drop us back off when we returned to town. That way we wouldn't have no trouble getting them towed or nothing. When we got back that night, Eddie pulled up on the curb about a quarter mile from where Paul was parked, and said, "All right, Paul, we're home."

Paul rose up and looked around. And since he could see cars, he got out and pulled his mandolin and Val-A-Pak out of the back. Then, once he started walking to where he thought his car was, we pulled way up the street, and Eddie stopped and turned his lights off so we could watch him. It was pretty comical. Paul would walk up one side of the street, he'd look and look, and then he'd walk across the other side of the street, and keep looking. Finally, Eddie said, "I feel for sorry for the poor old fat boy." So he turned around and picked him up. "I'm sorry, Paul," he said. "I made a mistake, your car's back up yonder." Poor old Paul never did know it was a joke. He always thought Eddie put him out accidentally.

Sometimes somebody'd get Eddie back, though, which was always good to see. Tony probably got him the best. See, Eddie always wanted to be a big tipper. If he had just a cup of coffee, he'd leave a dollar by way of tip if he could afford to. Finally, it got to where Tony couldn't take seeing him waste all that money, and he started picking it up after him. We used to go to this one restaurant right across from the radio station, and Tony picked up Eddie's tips for six months, putting them in a jar that he kept in the studio. It got to where the girls wouldn't wait on Eddie because they never got a tip from him.

One day he was griping about it in the studio. "I'm a damn good tipper," he was saying. "I don't understand what the hell's wrong with the waitresses over there."

Tony reached down on the floor and got that jar of money. "Here's what's wrong with the waitresses, Eddie," he said. "This is all the money you've been leaving on the table at that restaurant. They ain't got none of it."

Eddie wanted to whip him, but he was the backbone of his band, so there wasn't much he could do. But he had to quit eating at that place altogether, which made him even madder. Another thing about Eddie is that he was always tomcatting around. Bless his heart, he loved the ladies. It got to where he was buying apartments and cars for his girls. I can't even count how many times he'd tell us, "Y'all go on ahead, I'll meet you on the next date," and then he'd never show up. He'd stay in town in one of those apartments he was paying for and not go home for a week. And, of course, his wife would never know. She'd think he was just working on the road. She never had no idea where he was.

Besides being a sneak, Eddie also had very little respect for the law. If there was a handy place to park for the radio station, and the sign said that it was fifteen-minute parking, he'd park for two hours and just ignore the ticket. It finally got up to where he had two hundred and ten tickets, and one morning a gang of cops showed up at his house, banging on his door.

"Yes, officers?" Eddie said, answering the door.

"Eddie Hill?" the lead cop said.

"That's me."

"We have a warrant for your arrest for unpaid parking tickets."

Eddie laughed out loud. "Are you serious?"

"Yes, sir."

Eddie looked behind them and saw the cop cars. "Tell you what," he said. "I'm not riding in any of those pieces of shit. I'll let you follow me, but I'll drive down in my own damn car."

The cops all looked at one another, and they must have decided they didn't want to make this any harder than it was gonna be. One of the advantages of being as big as Eddie was that even cops thought twice before messing with him. "That's fine with us," the lead cop said.

"I'll fetch my keys," Eddie said, and slammed the door on them.

Well, he did fetch his keys. But he also put on his best suit and called his photographer, telling him that he'd be coming down to the jail. And when he got there, the photographer was waiting. He got two or three great pictures of Eddie cuffed, and gave them to *The Commercial Appeal*, which was the newspaper at the time. They ran it on the front page, "Smilin' Eddie Hill Arrested, Cops Claim He Owes on Over Two Hundred Parking Tickets."

Eddie paid a hundred dollars for all two hundred tickets. But, as he told me, "I couldn't have bought that space on the front page of the paper for five thousand dollars. Hell, I don't care what they say about me, as long as they spell my name right."

That was his way. He always insisted that if you want to be a star, then the first thing you have to do is look like a fucking star. If you look like a star and you act like a star, then you stand a chance. But if you look like a bum and call yourself a star, they're only gonna call you by the first name. You're just gonna be a bum.

CHAPTER 19

TUNESMITHS

Ira didn't really start writing songs seriously until we were in Memphis. We'd dabbled with songwriting a little, we even wrote out the words for one, but we didn't have any confidence in our ability to put a tune to it. We sent it off to one of those professional tunesmiths that advertised in the backs of magazines, but what we got back was so awful, we never tried it again.

But something about Memphis and working with Eddie Hill really seemed to put a match to Ira's creative side. He wrote at least thirty songs during that time, and with me helping to put a tune to them, we were playing 'em on the radio and really getting 'em out there. We even recorded one on the B-side of a record Smilin' Eddie Hill made for Apollo Records. It was a song called "Alabama" that Ira wrote about our home state. I'm pretty sure nobody ever knew about it but the engineer in the studio, but it was our first recording.

The problem was that if you don't know nobody, you couldn't get in to see nobody. Just like today. You have to know a big shot just to get anybody to listen. Well, we were complaining about that one day in the studio when Eddie happened to be in there, and he said, "You should have asked me, boys. I know a publisher. Put some of those songs on a reel-to-reel tape, and I'll take 'em up there for you."

"What publisher do you know, Eddie?" Ira asked. He looked a little skeptical. Neither of us had known Eddie to do much songwriting.

"Acuff-Rose," Eddie answered.

Well, hell, there was no way we could say no to that. Acuff-Rose was the publishing company owned by Fred Rose and Roy Acuff. We couldn't help but think of that big air-cooled Franklin, just imagining Roy Acuff getting to hear our songs. And Fred Rose was probably the best judge of a song in Nashville. He was the man behind Hank Williams, and one of the best songwriters of our time in his own right. He wrote, "I'll Never Get Out of This World Alive," "Blue Eyes Crying in the Rain," and a bunch of others that are standards now.

So we stayed in the studio for two days recording every song we had. And, as promised, when we got done, Eddie took them off to Fred Rose. I'll tell you about nervous. Some people seemed to like our songs when we played them on the radio or at a show, but we had no idea if they were any good at all. I doubt either of us slept for two days after turning them over to Eddie.

I was probably more worried for Ira's sake than my own. He was the kind who couldn't take any criticism at all. If I told him that I thought changing one little thing might make a song better, he'd be liable not to talk to me for a day. If he got it in his head you'd insulted him, he could brood like no man I ever met. There wasn't nothing to do but stay out of his way when he got like that. If you didn't, he'd cut you right in half with a word or two. He never shied from letting me know how my guitar playing measured up to his mandolin. Nor how little he thought I brought to the writing.

But then we got word that Fred loved the songs, and that he wanted to sign us to a recording contract. We were thrilled. The way we figured it, as professional Nashville songwriters we were only a year or two from the Opry.

But then we learned that Eddie had put all the songs down as being written by "Smilin' Eddie Hill and the Louvin Brothers." This meant that half our royalties was going to Eddie Hill. We tried to grin and bear it, because we had no idea if we could object and maintain our job, but it was awfully hard to stomach.

So the next time we had a batch of songs ready to go, we didn't ask Eddie for any help. Instead, I called up Fred Rose and asked him if he'd mind if we just dropped them by his office.

"You don't have to come all the way out here every time you got a song," he said. "I'll give you my address, and you can just send the lead sheets to me."

"I'm sorry, Mr. Rose," I said. "Neither Ira nor I can read or write music." Boy, did I feel like a dumbass. It was hard not to think of those singing school classes that Papa had tried to get us to take.

"Ah," he said. "I understand. That's the way with Hank, too. Well, when can you make it up to Nashville?"

"That's the other thing," I said. "We pretty much only have one day off a week, and it's Sunday. Every other day we're either playing a show or on the road to one."

"That's no problem, son," he said. "The next Sunday you have free and you have a song, you just stop by my house and ring the bell."

So the next time we had songs ready to go, that's what we

did. As soon as we got back to Memphis that Saturday night, Ira and I threw our stuff in the car and lit out for Nashville.

We didn't get to Fred's house until around seven in the morning, and I can only imagine what a mess we must have looked. Neither of us had changed clothes after Saturday night's show, and I hadn't slept in nearly two days for driving. For his part, Ira was stepping back and forth on his feet, trying to keep the back pain away. But Fred answered the door right away, took one look at us, and said, "Hello, boys. Good to see you." Only seven in the morning, and he was already dressed in a fresh suit, with his thinning hair combed back. He was only about my height, paunchy, and not a real impressive figure, but he had this real intense way of looking at you, like he was trying to peer straight through your skull into your brain. It was unnerving as hell.

Ira stuck out his hand and gave him his most charming smile. "I hope we're not too early, Mr. Rose," he said.

"No, of course not," Fred said. "Let's go around back to my studio."

His studio was a little building out back that he'd stocked full of all this powerful expensive equipment that meant nothing to him, including a studio quality reel-to-reel tape recorder. He set it up and said, "All right, boys, whenever you're ready."

We laid into our first song. Of course, we'd rehearsed and rehearsed every one of them, until we could play them perfect from start to finish. Ira made sure of that. When it came to music, he had no use for sloppiness whatsoever. But the pills I'd taken to keep me awake had given me a headache big enough for an Army. God, my head was just busting from lack of sleep. And, finally, after two or three songs, I said, "Mr. Fred, do you have any aspirin?"

"Aspirin," he said, peering at me like a mole. "What's that?"

I thought he was fooling with me. "I've got a terrible headache," I said. "Do you have anything for a headache?"

"No," he said, "I don't have anything for a headache. Not here."

I still didn't understand. "You never get a headache?" I asked.

"Do I look stupid enough to want my head to hurt?" he answered.

"Naw, I don't mean that," I said, "But my head is hurting. I don't think I did anything to cause it, but I need something to stop it."

"Well, I don't keep any medicine in the house," he said.

I had no idea what was going on. I'd never met anyone who didn't take medicine when they needed it, but I knew I needed something bad. "How's about a drugstore?" I asked. "Is there a drugstore anywhere around here?"

"I think there's one down the road," he said. "I've never been in there."

"All right," I said. "I'll be right back."

So I ran down to the drugstore and got the medicine. And when I got back, we finished the session, and he took every one of the songs.

About ten minutes after we left Fred's house, driving on our way back to Memphis, Ira started giggling. I mean giggling like a little girl. And then guffawing, slapping the dashboard.

"What are you laughing at?" I asked. The headache had receded some, but I still wasn't very much in a jolly mood.

"I wish you could have seen your face when he asked you if he looked stupid enough to get a headache," he said.

"Who ever heard of somebody not keeping aspirin in the house?" I grumbled.

"He's a weirdo, man," Ira said. "A Seventh Day Adventist. He don't believe in medicine of any kind. Thinks it goes against God's will. That's why he looks at you like that, too. He's blind as a bat, but won't get glasses."

"How do you know all that?" I asked.

"Eddie told me. I guess I should have told you, too."

"I guess you should have."

"But then I wouldn't have got to see your face, would I?"

Ira, Smilin' Eddie, and me

CHAPTER 20

HONEYMOON

One Sunday after I'd been hanging around Betty's all day, her daddy came out on the porch where we were sitting, took one look at us, and said, "Don't you think it's time y'all got married?"

I'd been thinking about it for some time, actually, but I knew I couldn't ask her to marry me until I got a raise. She made thirty-four dollars a week, and for most of our courting, I was only making twenty dollars a week from Eddie Hill. I didn't want to marry her making less than she did. But just a few days before her daddy said that, I'd finally gotten a raise. A doublin' raise, too, to forty dollars a week. And I'd even bought her a ring. But I was storing it in a rich woman's safety deposit box until I got up the nerve to pop the question, and that woman was out of town.

Still, I couldn't let an opportunity like that get away, so I just came out with it. "Betty, I think he's right. Let's get married."

I'll never forget her response. "Okay, I guess," is what she said. It wasn't the strongest answer I'd ever heard, but it was awful welcome, anyway. So we told her father, and he gave us eight dollars for the preacher, which is what it cost.

I had a show that night, and I brought her with me. At the time, Floyd "Lightnin' " Chance was in our band. I borrowed his wife's ring, and Betty and I got married in Hernando, Mississippi, with Lightnin' as our witness. We walked up to the preacher's house and he hitched us right there. There wasn't a single picture taken, but it was memorable enough for me without 'em. A lot of folks feel they have to have a professional photographer and a thousand dollars worth of pictures, but that's not necessary for a marriage.

Betty and me, just married

I was twenty-two years old when I married her. And the truth is I wouldn't have married her before I did, even if I'd already had the raise. See, I remembered that conversation Papa and I had at the woodpile so many years ago, about how dumb my sisters were for marrying so young. Years after I married Betty I reminded Papa of that, too. He just kind of laughed and said, "Aw, you know I was just kidding." But I don't think he was.

Papa loved Betty, though. And Mama did, too. In fact, after Mama got Alzheimer's, she knew Betty for four years longer than she knew me. We'd go in her room in the nursing home to visit her, and the second Betty walked in the door, Mama'd say, "Little Betty." She didn't know me from Adam, though, and that hurt a little. You got to be a real asshole for your own Mama not to know you. But she always knew Betty, and I was always grateful for that.

Anyway, just a couple days after our marriage I talked Betty into going with us to another show, joking that it'd be our honeymoon. I wasn't planning on making a habit of taking her on the road because I knew the rules, but I drove my own car, and she wasn't a burden on anybody. The show was in Bald Knob, Arkansas, and I drove Ira, Betty, and Sonny James in my little Studebaker, and then Eddie was behind us in his Cadillac limousine with the rest of the band being driven by Tony.

Well, on the way back from the show, we ran into this place where the road bisected. You had to turn right, go less than a block, and then cut left to stay on course. And right next to that left turn was a Dairy Queen. So we took that turn, and I was going down the highway maybe seventy miles an hour when I saw Eddie's lights start coming up on my left in the passing lane.

Tony loved to show off his driving, and it used to get on my nerves a little. "If Tony's crazy enough to try to outrun me with that Cadillac limo, he's gonna have to get on it," I said, and I hit the gas. But he stepped on his, too, and pulled right up on me. There was no way I was gonna let him pass, so I hit the gas again, pushed it up to about ninety-five miles an hour, and pulled away. Then I slowed a little, just toying with him, and let him catch up.

I did that four or five times before I said, "Tony don't care if he tears up that Cadillac limo because it ain't his, but if I tear this car up, I'll be the one to pay for it." So I tapped the brakes one time, enough to let the tail lights come on and signal that he could pass.

The sonofagun pulled right up on me, not three feet away, and I looked over there fixing to shoot him the finger, and there was a damn siren on the right front fender. It was a cop car.

Lordy mercy, I knew I was screwed. And sure enough, when I pulled over they didn't even ask if anybody else could drive the car. They just took me right out from behind the wheel, put me in the backseat of the cop car, and made a U-turn.

But just before they could get started back to town, here comes Eddie's car, Tony driving. Turns out they'd stopped in the Dairy Queen back at that left turn to get something to eat. Tony damn near run over them cops, but he got the Cadillac stopped, and Eddie rolled his window down. "What's happening, officer?"

"Keep driving or I'll run your ass in, too," the cop said.

"Hey, germ," Eddie said, "if you got something to say to me, say it with a little dignity." He'd have probably got out and punched that cop in the face if the cop had said one more word, but the cop didn't. So Tony made a U-turn in the Cadillac and Ira made a U-turn in my car, and everybody followed us back to town.

As we drove, I gave the cops my story. I told them I'd just got married the day before yesterday, which was true, that

I thought his car was Eddie Hill's car, which was also true, and that I'm not in the habit of trying to outrun cops, which was definitely true. All the while I was talking, I was also working the forty dollars I had in my pocket down into my boot, because I'd always heard the Arkansas cops weren't above taking whatever money you had on you.

I think I had 'em softened up pretty good by the time we got back to the station. I believe they were fixing to just give me a good pep talk and let me go. But then Tony came in. He was a little Italian, black hair greased back, about five foot tall, with a huge mouth. And the first thing he said was, "I bet you wish you was driving Eddie's Continental instead of that little Studebaker, don't you, Charlie? They wouldn't have caught you then, would they?"

Well, that just fucked up the whole case. It made it sound like I made a habit of trying to outrun cops wherever I went. So they fined me ninety dollars, which was two weeks pay. Luckily, Eddie was there, and he paid to keep me out of the jug.

CHAPTER 21

DECCA

The good times with Eddie couldn't last forever. Nothing does. Around 1949, Ira and I were starting to figure Memphis was getting played out. It was just like every town before. We'd done every venue that was big enough to hold a show two or three times over, and that's just about all people will put up with from you. They won't come to see the same program over and over.

We also didn't have a record contract, and we knew that was killing us. So we did the only thing we could think to do. We asked Fred Rose if he knew anybody in Nashville he could talk to about getting us a record cut. We figured it was to his advantage, really. Other artists were starting to record the songs we published with Acuff-Rose, and for every dollar we made, he made ten.

It worked, too. Fred managed to get us a half session with Decca, which was the home of Ernest Tubb, the Texas Troubadour, among others. We cut "Alabama" again since

the folks at Decca figured nobody'd ever heard the Apollo version we'd done, and then recorded a new song called the "Seven Year Blues," which was a waltz.

But the deal just died there. We wanted to record more, but the producer with Decca, Paul Cohen, was sending us bullshit. I mean you couldn't put harmony to that stuff at all. We kept trying to tell him that we had more songs than we could possibly perform, and they were written specifically for harmony, but he informed us that we were gonna cut whatever he sent. So every time they set up a session, one of us would get sick and we'd skip it altogether. We did it all year, until the contract ran out and we didn't have to get sick no more.

Then, to make things worse, we caught wind that Eddie Hill was planning to leave for Nashville, where he had a radio show lined up with WSM, home of the Opry. He hadn't announced it or anything, just a rumor we heard, but it sounded likely. We got a little depressed about our chances in Memphis then. The town had been awfully good to us, but with the shows slowing down and no Eddie Hill, there was no good reason to stay.

Then, just as we were starting to wonder if we'd ever be able to support ourselves again, we got an offer to come back to Knoxville. Lowell Blanchard, who was one of the most famous radio presenters in country music at the time, told us he'd give us two hundred dollars a week to star in his Midday Merry-Go-Round and Tennessee Barn Dance. Hell, with Eddie, we never made more than eighty dollars together, so there was no way we could pass that up. Besides which, everybody knew that Lowell Blanchard's shows were a training ground for the Opry. And that's still all we really wanted to do.

Of course, we were broke when we rolled into town. It was a tough time. The whole band lived with us, and Betty was supporting us all. And since Ira was always taking off with my car for his dates, Betty and I had to either sit around the house or ride the bus into town for a movie. Not that Ira was alone in tomcattin' around. Our fiddle player, Paige Hepler, wouldn't rehearse in the house unless I put something black over the windows. He was scared the father of the girl he was dating would come shoot him through the window. But we figured at two hundred a week, it wouldn't be no time before we each had our own house. And then they could black out their own windows.

Blanchard was something. A real showman. He had us doing recitations, comedy, everything. For a little while, he even had Ira dressed up in a bonnet and a gingham dress. And he gave him this instrument made out of a washboard, bicycle horns, bells, a coon tail, and an owl's head that he called a

Betty and me

hootenanny. It was ridiculous, if you want my opinion, but folks seemed to like it.

Then, one day we were up onstage singing a song, and Ira's mandolin got out of tune. It'll happen with mandolins easier than any other instrument. They got eight strings and only four sounds, and unless all the strings are just exactly as new as all the other strings, it won't note true. Ira tried to fix it, but he just couldn't get it in tune. So he slung it clear back against the backdrop, and then went back and stomped it into shivers.

Naturally, the audience thought that was part of the show. They thought it was great. You'd hear 'em yelling out, "You got anything else you can stomp?" You could probably take a crap onstage and there'd be people in the audience who thought it was funny. You got people like that everywhere.

It was something Ira'd done before, getting mad at one of his mandolins. He never was real good at controlling his temper, and nothing pissed him off like an out of tune instrument. But he'd never done it right there in front of everybody. Still, there wasn't time to gawk over it, as we were in the middle of the song, so me and the guitar player finished it out.

It wasn't a second after the last note died off before we got word that Mr. Lowell Blanchard wanted to see us in the office, and now. He didn't beat around the bush when we got in there, neither. "That was an extremely amateurish thing to do, Ira," he said.

"It's my mandolin," Ira said. "I'll stomp it if I want to."

"I'll let it go once," Lowell said. "But if it ever happens again, you won't have to come see me, you can just consider yourselves fired."

Well, I knew how well Ira responded to threats. I had no doubt that the next time he was onstage, he'd smash his mandolin just to let Blanchard know he didn't take orders from anybody. It was as if Papa had used up all the tolerance Ira had for being told what to do. There was no good deal he wouldn't screw up just to tell somebody "fuck you" that he thought deserved it.

So I did what I always had to do when I could foresee one of Ira's coming storms. I started hunting for another place to work. And I finally found us a spot on a barn dance show in Greensboro, North Carolina. For a little while it looked like we were gonna be fine, too. But then that job petered out, and we had to move on to Danville, Virginia, to another show. The salary was only fifty dollars a week for the both of us, and even with booking all the shows we could handle, Betty still had to work to support us.

And then things went from bad to worse. Having just divorced one useless woman, Ira decided it was time to marry another. And with all of us sharing the same house. Her name was Bobbie Lowery, and it didn't take long for them to start fighting just like he and Annie Lou had done.

CHAPTER 22

HANK WILLIAMS

We did have one good stroke of luck during that dark time. Or, at least, we thought it was gonna be a stroke of luck when it first happened. Somehow, Fred Rose got us another record contract, this time with MGM. It was a young label and Fred was the one who'd brought Hank Williams to it, so I guess he could do whatever he wanted.

We recorded a few songs with MGM. We even tried to get a waltz out, "The Get Acquainted Waltz." At the time, Patti Page's "Tennessee Waltz" was probably the biggest thing going. A good waltz takes time to catch on with the public, but once it does, it'll never die. Ours didn't do a damn thing, though.

It was at the MGM studios that I first saw Hank Williams. We were supposed to record at ten o'clock one night, and Ira and I got stuck behind Lonzo and Oscar, who were poor copycats of another duet, Homer and Jethro. Very poor copycats, as it turned out. They were trying to cut a song called "Who

Pulled the Plug from the Jug," which was simple enough, but they worked on it until twelve thirty or one o'clock in the morning, and still couldn't get it. Finally, around one thirty they gave up, and Ira and I got in there. We were just getting tuned up, but before we could start recording, Hank Williams rolled in for his twelve o'clock appointment.

He was drunk as a pissant, his arm around a real knockout. It was Billy Jean, as it turned out, the one he married for his second wife. Fred, who was there to watch over our session, jumped up to meet him. "Hang on, chief," he told Hank. "We ain't quite ready for you yet."

"Am I early?" Hank asked.

"By about twenty-three hours," Fred said, "but we'll take care of you as soon as I get these boys recorded."

"I'll wait," Hank said, and when he turned to find a place to sit down, we all saw that he had bills, hundred-dollar bills, just hanging out of his pockets.

"You're fixing to go broke, Chief," Fred said. He pulled a pencil out of his pocket and pushed the bills back into Hank's pocket.

Well, Billy Jean just about peed herself laughing, but Hank waved Fred away. "Hell, boy," he said, "there's plenty more where those came from."

We went ahead and recorded our session, which lasted a total of eleven minutes. They were songs that we'd done so many times that even Ira agreed they were perfect on the first take. And as soon as we were done, we said our adieus and vamoosed out of there.

I saw Hank one more time, not that much later. Ira and I went to play the Louisiana Hayride in Shreveport, with a couple hours off between the first and second show, so we were fixing to walk across the street to this little old restaurant they had across from the Shreveport Municipal Memorial Auditorium. We stepped off the curb, and I saw a man lying by the sidewalk, dead drunk, puke running about five feet from his head down to the gutter.

"Who in the shit is that?" I asked Ira.

"That's Hank Williams," Ira said, scorn in his voice.

And it was. He had just got so drunk he couldn't make it from the Hayride over to the restaurant. It was tragic to see. A man with the ability, talent, and future like the one he had, to see him waste it on the bottle.

I believe writers are born writers of music. I don't believe anyone can teach you how to write a song. If you weren't born to write, you'll never write anything worth passing along. And if you ask me, Hank was one of the two greatest songwriters of our time. And the other, Ira, he became a real drinker, too.

The thing about Hank Williams was that he wasn't any better a writer than my brother was, he just wrote about different things. Hank was always leaving a woman or just getting back from being gone, so that's what he wrote about. Ira wrote about choices. When he wrote the gospel songs, he didn't preach fire and brimstone, but he'd explain the choices to you. If you're a pretty decent guy, you'll go up. But if you're an asshole, then you'll go down. And that's your choice. That's all we ever sang about.

I always got the feeling that some of those songs came from Ira understanding that he should have been a preacher, that maybe he'd made the wrong choice himself. From an early age, he was a regular prodigy when it came to scripture. He could recite chapter and verse of almost anything in the Bible, too. He knew it all. And when he testified, the spirit of the Lord came upon him. Even when he was a kid, the whole church fell silent to hear him. There wasn't a person on Sand Mountain who didn't think he was gonna be a preacher when he grew up. Mama was very proud of him, especially since her father was a preacher. I don't think there's anything in the world that she wouldn't have given for Ira to be like his grandfather.

So I never could understand the drinking. Not with Hank, and not with Ira, either. Whiskey don't cure nothing. You might forget what you're trying to forget tonight, but when you wake up tomorrow, it'll be back. And so will your headache and hangover. It'll just multiply on you, and eventually whiskey won't do any good at all for what you're trying to use it for. Whether it be to forget or to have a good time, there'll come a day when it'll require more than you can drink, more than anybody can drink. And that will be your complete downfall. That's what happened to Hank. It got to where the whiskey couldn't do him any good, so he had to move on to something stronger.

I've talked to the guy who was driving when Hank died in the backseat of that Cadillac on the way to Canton, Ohio. Hank hadn't slept in days and he told the driver, "I've got to have some sleep, man. I can't sleep. Let's go through Knoxville." So they pulled through Knoxville, and he called that doctor up and told him, "I have got to have some sleep. I just have to." I don't know what he was on, but he couldn't go to sleep without help.

Sure enough, that doctor gave him a shot and it worked. Hank wanted some sleep, and he's still sleeping.

CHAPTER 23

CAPITOL RECORDS

None of our records with MGM hit at all, and once again, things were starting to look real bleak. Fred finally told us what the deal was. "I made a mistake putting you on MGM," was how he put it. "If your name's not Hank Williams or Patti Page, you don't need to be there. That's where all their promotion money goes."

That tore it. Our dream of being on the Opry was starting to look so remote neither Ira nor I could think of any way we might actually reach it. I'm almost ashamed to admit it, but we started to explore other options. We still kept the act going somewhat, but we gave up being full-time musicians. I got a job working at the Post Office, and started going to barber college on the GI Bill. Ira and Bobbie moved down to Knoxville to be closer to her people, and he took a job at one of Cas Walker's stores as a grocery clerk.

When I look back on my career, that was probably the most dangerous point. I don't believe in quitting, and I don't believe in being lazy, but right then it looked like there was nothing we could do to make our dream work for us.

But then, we had just one more stroke of good luck. Just a small one. One day my boss at the Post Office told me that he thought he could get Ira a job as a temporary employee, and even as a temporary employee he'd make more than he was making as a grocery clerk. Of course, Ira didn't have a phone at the time, so as soon as I got off work that night, Betty and I jumped in the car and drove some three hundred and fifty miles down to Knoxville to give him the news.

Somehow, he talked Bobbie into coming back to Memphis and taking the job, so he came on as a substitute mail clerk. He stayed a substitute his whole career with the Post Office, too. He just could not pass the common sense test to become full time to save his life. Ira had many gifts, but common sense never was one of them.

With that move to Memphis, something else happened in our favor. Somehow, we managed to get our own show at WMPS. Just a little show, not nearly enough to pay the bills, of course, but it kept us in the business. And then, after a couple months of working at WMPS, we got a call from Fred Rose. He'd stuck his neck out for us one more time, and it was the break that we needed. He'd called up Ken Nelson, who was the head of country music for Capitol Records, and landed us a third recording contract.

At the time, all of Capitol's folks stayed in California, so the first couple sessions we didn't really have an A&R man. Fred had to step in and take over himself. He scheduled our first studio session at the Tulane Hotel, and lined up all of our musicians, including Chet Atkins, who worked all those early sessions. Chet Atkins went on to become one of the most famous record producers who ever lived, helping to create the Nashville Sound, but at the time, he was known as one of the best session guitarists in town.

Man, when I walked into the studio, I about tore Fred's

hand off shaking it, I was so happy with what he'd done. And then I did a double take. He was wearing glasses. Big ones, too. The lenses looked like the bottom of a pair of pop bottles.

"What do you got there, Fred?" I asked.

"Oh, these." He fiddled with the glasses on his nose. "Roy made me start wearing 'em. Said he wouldn't be in business with a blind man."

Well, I tried not to laugh. But it made him a lot easier to work with, now that he could actually see. I always wished Fred would've taken the lesson learned from those glasses and applied it to other areas as well. Poor man didn't last much longer. He died in 1954, and he could've lived decades longer if he only would've taken a blood pressure pill. But he didn't believe in pills, and so it goes.

The one downside to the Capitol Records deal was that we

Finally, a record deal

signed as a gospel-only act. They already had a secular duet, Jim and Jesse McReynolds, and they told us in no uncertain terms that they didn't need another. The funny thing was that Jim and Jesse got their contract with Capitol by singing one of our secular songs, "Are You Missing Me?" But, hell, we needed a contract bad, so we didn't raise no fuss. From 1952 to 1955, we recorded nothing but gospel, making do the best we could.

Our first Capitol record was two songs we'd written: "The Family Who Prays" paired with "Let Us Travel, Travel On." It must've done better than we expected, because about three months after that first session, we got a check in the mail for $596 from Ken Nelson.

I actually had no idea what the check was for, so I called up Ken Nelson. I'd still never met him, but I had talked to him on the phone a couple times.

"Hello, Charlie," he said. "What can I do for you?"

Capitol Artists, 1953

"I think somebody out there made a mistake, Mr. Nelson, sir," I said. "We got a check here in the mail for five hundred, ninety-six dollars that looks like it came from you."

He laughed out loud. "Haven't you ever heard of mechanical royalties, Charlie?"

Lord, did I feel stupid. But we'd never gotten a penny from MGM, so I guess it was natural.

Now that we had a real recording contract that looked like it was gonna last, it seemed like it was time we got on the Opry. So Ira and I decided to start auditioning whenever we could. We didn't know how you got on the Opry, but we figured there couldn't be nothing to it. So we just drove to Nashville one day and walked in the Ryman Auditorium looking for somebody to sing to.

There were musicians and pickers standing around everywhere, talking and strumming. The Fruit Jar Drinkers, The Gully Jumpers, all kinds of bands. We just grabbed some dude and asked him who the man in charge was, and he pointed us at Jim Denny. Seeing him, it made sense. For one thing, he was the only one backstage wearing a three-piece suit and a hat. He just had that look about him, as if it were all his show to run, sliding his glasses down his long nose and watching everybody over the top of them. We went over to Denny and told him we had a couple songs we'd really like him to hear, and he agreed to take a listen. At the time, they had a shed in the old Ryman Auditorium where they stored all the tools to keep the curtains and bathrooms operating. It was about the only place you could go to get out of standing in the middle of a crowd of people. So we went in there where we'd have fewer distractions and played two songs for him.

"Thanks, but no thanks," he said as soon as we'd finished, sliding out of the toolshed. He didn't even hesitate.

But we kept trying. If we got a Saturday night off, we'd hightail it to Nashville, wiggle our way through the alley entrance into the Opry, and trick Jim Denny into going into the toolshed with us. But he kept giving us that same shit, "Don't call us, we'll call you." And the call never came. I'm pretty sure he was stringing us along to keep us out of everybody's hair.

The dream of the Opry kept slipping further and further away with every one of those rejections. It meant the world to us, but it was dimming. In a way, I'm surprised we kept trying. We thought about giving up more times than I can count, but I don't even think we knew how. Giving up meant accepting some things we couldn't accept. It meant that Papa was right, that the way he lived was the only way to live. He loved music, but was always on us whenever we went home to visit. "When are you boys gonna settle down and get a real job?" he'd ask. "You've had your fun, but this ain't no life for grown men with a family."

If I was looking at someone else with the career path we had, I'd have probably told them to let it go at that point. I don't know how long you should keep trying if you don't seem to be making any progress. There comes a time when you just have to say, "I've given it my best and it wasn't good enough." But we never could do that.

CHAPTER 24

THE
24TH
INFANTRY DIVISION
BOOTLEGGERS

It was just about then that I got one of the biggest surprises of my life. I come home one day after my shift at the Post Office and found a draft notice in the mail. They were looking to send me to Korea. I couldn't hardly believe it. I'd already done my time, and to top it off, Betty was pregnant. I marched straight down to the recruitment office to tell them how stupid they were. "You're insane," I told the recruiting officer. "I've already done everything I was supposed to do."

"No, you haven't," he said, reading over the letter. "You've only served fourteen months active duty, and the requirement is twenty-four. That makes you subject to the draft."

"What about my wife?" I said. "She's pregnant. I can't just leave her."

"Sure you can," he said. "She can have a baby just as well with you in Korea as she could if you were here."

That pissed me off, but there wasn't nothing I could do about it. The recruiter sent me to the Red Cross, where they told me to have my wife call 'em when she had the baby, and they'd let me know within twenty-four hours. Which was bullshit. When my boy Sonny was born, Betty notified the Red Cross it was a boy, but, just in case, she also had her sister write me a letter. I got the letter about three weeks after it was mailed, and two or three days after that I got the call from the Red Cross. My opinion of them hasn't risen any since.

I didn't get to test the recruitment officer's words with my second boy, either. Ira and I were in Minneapolis doing a week's set at the Flame Supper Club when he was born. Of course, I burned up the phone lines when I found out Betty'd gone to the hospital, but I missed it completely.

I did finally learn he was dead right, though. It hurts to

My sons: Sonny, Glenn, and Ken

admit it, but he was. I was lucky enough to be in town for the birth of my third boy, and there wasn't nothing in the world I could do. They put me in a room, and I sat there wringing my hands until they had him cleaned up and in the nursery. I almost wished I was back in Korea at that point. I tried to get something out of every damn nurse that walked out, but they played like they didn't know nothing.

Anyway, there was nothing I could do but go to Korea. So I shipped out in a Merchant Marine ship the same as everybody else. Almost didn't make it neither. We went through a hurricane in the Pacific that nearly sunk us all. The waters were so rough that it actually broke the boat. Not completely in two, but enough that it leaked. We just managed to coast into Yokohama, Japan, and we had to change boats to go on to Pusan, Korea, where I was supposed to unload.

Then, I don't know how it happened, but I got tangled up with some Marines and ended up on a train somewhere fifty miles north of the 38th parallel. You could hear the guns going and see the casualties. I'll tell you what, if you ever end up in a place like that, you'll be ready to get away. But when you got thousands of miles of water between there and where you want to be, it cuts out an awful lot of your options.

I got lucky, though, and they didn't have a place to use me up there, so I got on the same train and went back to Pusan where they put me on a boat, and I shipped off to Koje-Do island, where all the Korean prisoners were kept.

It turned out to be a pretty good place to be, as places in Korea go. There wasn't too much fighting, and somehow I ended up working in the APO, the Army Post Office, which was right up my alley. The hardest I had it was getting woke up early now and then. Officers would step off a helicopter at maybe two thirty or three o'clock in the morning, and they'd come down to my tent, calling out, "Loudermilk! I need to pick up my mail!"

So I'd get out of bed, put on my fatigues, and walk bare-footed to the tent, which was like fifty or seventy-five feet away, and get their mail for them out of their cubbyhole. There never was a one of them that didn't say, "If there's ever anything over here that you could use my help with, you make sure to call me."

Well, I didn't germ 'em, and I didn't even ask 'em for many favors. But a couple times when the action was low, and there was a helicopter vacant, one of them would take me up and fly me around like I was a big shot. That meant a lot to me. It got me away from all things in a war that you don't need to be around twenty-four hours a day.

I couldn't think of a thing in the world that we were supposed to be fighting for in Korea, if you want the truth. So I chose smoking cigarettes. I just pretended that if we lost, whomever we lost to was gonna do away with smoking altogether. I couldn't think of anything that made anymore sense than that, so that's what I stuck with. I figured surely there must be one thing that I could say that I fought for.

Of course, they've about done away with smoking now right here at home. California's the worst at it. They'll pass some stupid law restricting your privileges, and the other 49 states'll say, "Aw shit, why didn't we think of that? We gotta pass that, too." It's gotten to where you gotta keep your privileges kind of rolled up and tucked in your pocket. You can't let nobody know what rights you think you have, because sooner or later they'll find a way to take 'em from you.

The only other thing that made Korea tolerable was that Jesse McReynolds, half of Capitol's secular duet, Jim and Jesse, was over there, too. His job was to make donuts and coffee for the troops. Every morning, they would take a pretty good-size two-ton truck, fill it with about a ton-and-a-half of donuts and a couple hundred gallons of coffee, and drive it around in the fields, so the Red Cross girls could share it with the troops. All the troops were sure that those girls had stayed up all night making those donuts and that coffee, but it wasn't them. The reason they looked so tired and haunty had nothing to do with baking donuts. They were staying up all night servicing the officers.

They made plenty of money at it, too, some of those Red Cross girls. I knew all about it, because I was mailing their money home for them. They could only stay over there twelve months, and when it came time to head home, Lord, but they'd cry and carry on for the Army to keep 'em another year because of all they were doing for the troops. But the truth was they couldn't afford to leave the money they made from the officers.

We played together, Jesse and me. We called ourselves The Dusty Roads Boys because there wasn't twenty feet of blacktop in Korea. We worked officer's clubs, mainly. They wouldn't pay us nothing, because we already had Army pay, but if we worked an officer's club each of us could choose from a case of beer or a fifth of A-grade bourbon.

The bourbon came in handy. This one officer came from Atlanta, Georgia, and he was a serious drinker. He would always, and I mean always, go out on a Saturday night and get completely wiped out. Every Saturday night, somebody would have to carry him home after he passed out, and he'd wake up every Sunday morning with no way to buy whiskey. So every single Sunday around midday, he'd send his runner to my tent. "The Captain sent me down here to see if you had a fifth," the runner'd say. "It don't make no difference what brand it is, as long as it hasn't been opened."

"Sure, I got one," I'd say.

"What do you want for it?"

"Twenty-five dollars."

And so every Sunday morning the Captain would buy the fifth I'd worked for at whatever club Jesse and I played at.

The Dusty Roads Boys in Korea

I asked him once why he didn't buy another bottle for Sunday, and he said, "Hell, if I bought another bottle for Sunday, it wouldn't last through Saturday night. I'd just drink it, too."

Nobody seemed to want beer at all, so I never trifled with that. But I sold the whiskey to the same man, every Sunday morning. And I guess that makes me one of the 24th Infantry Division Bootleggers.

CHAPTER 25

BUSBOYS

Everybody had to find some way to pass the time over there. Jesse and I played music, but some of the other guys found other things better suited to them. Like spending their money on what they liked to call busboys. Only they weren't boys, they were Korean girls. They just happened to look exactly like boys, short hair and totally titless. The guys'd give 'em five dollars a week to keep their boots shined and their clothes ironed with an edge on it so it would almost cut you. And so that they'd screw 'em at night.

Those kinds of deals were always available, but I never touched 'em. I'll admit those girls did start looking a little better after a while, but they weren't for me. I always felt it was mean of them to throw it in my face when I couldn't have it, but I was married, which is as it should be. As long as you can hold out, anyway.

I only stayed over there ten months. I wrote everybody and his dog trying to get out. The person I wrote the most was

Sen. Estes Kefauver. I knew he was a pretty good senator, and, finally, one day I got a letter from him that said, "Go to your company commander and show them this letter. You've been in ten months, which, added to your fourteen, makes twenty-four months active duty. As of right now you're eligible for discharge."

Buddy, I ran down there and gave them that letter. And within two days, I was on orders to ship back home. It was a surprise homecoming. I never did tell Betty I was coming, because I wanted to make sure it was absolutely settled before I got her hopes up. And then, when I did finally work it out, I ended up getting home a day before the letter I wrote telling 'em to expect me. I was discharged at the airbase outside of Denver, and then had to ride a slow train to Chicago, another

Betty and me with our sons Sonny and Glenn

slower train to Chattanooga, and then a bus to Memphis, and I still beat the letter.

Bless her heart, Betty was happy to see me. I called her from the bus station and she came and got me with Sonny in tow. I couldn't believe how big he was. The first words out of my mouth were, "Good Lord, you said we had a baby!"

"Well, he is, Charlie," she said. "He's only three months old."

It was a joyous time, though I had to teach Sonny to trust me, that I wasn't there to steal him or do anything to hurt him. You'd be surprised to know how much a three-month-old has already learned. They know right off who their carekeepers are, and who might or might not hurt them. It was kind of funky while we got to know each other, but it's worked like a greased machine since.

Looking back on it, I don't feel good about that whole Korean war at all. I'd have to lie big time to tell you I wasn't afraid, because I had some close, close friends that were sent over there, and thirty days later, they didn't exist anymore. And there were a lot of people that got killed in the areas I was in. I felt twenty-four-carat lucky to be in the APO, where we had no weapons and we weren't trying to bother anybody. We were just there to keep people happy by receiving their mail. That's all.

But even doing that, I still got called a baby-killing bastard when I got back. Of course, I wasn't. I sure as hell didn't want to be there, in Korea. But I was sent, I did what I was told, and I was not told to kill no babies, nor mothers carrying babies, so I didn't.

The worst thing was that Korea was the reason I voted Republican for the first time. I voted for Eisenhower because he said, "If you elect me, I'll bring the boys home from Korea." What he didn't say in his speech was, "I've gotta send some more of you boys over there to help bring 'em back." That's where I got screwed right there. It pissed me off to no end what he did, I'll tell you that.

The fact is that nobody wins in a war. A lot of people lose, but nobody wins. Like in Vietnam, they finally signed an agreement to disagree and that's the way we left. Not as victors, but more as somebody that shouldn't have been there. We cannot change the world.

Course beliefs are just like assholes, everybody's got one, but I think it's the same thing in Afghanistan. You can't change people who have been that way for six thousand years. That's what we're trying to do, change their religion, change their thinking, change everything. It seems like the United States thinks that money will do it, but nothing changes people but time. And even then, it ain't always for the best.

CHAPTER 26

KEN NELSON

While I was in Korea, Ira held down a spot as a DJ on a little radio program on WMPS, and as soon as I got back, we started playing again. We'd already had to start over twice before thanks to Uncle Sam, but our time with Smilin' Eddie Hill had been one of the most profitable of our career, and we'd somehow managed to forget about all the lean years before and after. We had no doubt that this time we'd make it.

We were two determined little bastards. If we did something and it didn't work, we just told ourselves we'd done it wrong, and tried to do it better next time. We were no good at quitting at all. Whether or not he meant to, I'd say that's one of the greatest gifts Papa gave us.

Besides being a disc jockey, Ira was still working at the Post Office. Well, pretty much the first day after getting back from Korea, I was ready to go down there and get my job back. By that time, I had been voted a full-fledged civil servant, and I knew I only had thirty days after discharge to get my job back if I wanted to keep it. But Ira called me up on the telephone before I could make the trip. "I've got something I need to talk you about," he said. "I think I found us a gig."

"Where at?" I asked.

"Birmingham."

"Birmingham, Alabama?"

"I don't know any other Birmingham."

"Aw, shit, Ira," I said. "You know nobody does good in their own state."

"Not this time," he said. "We're gonna make a killing."

I had that sinking feeling I got whenever I knew he was gonna talk me into something. "Tell me about it," I said.

"I've been talking to the people at WVOK," he said. "They'll pay us a hundred dollars a week, sponsor money. We'll sell a lot of baby chicks and shit like that, and the show dates will be phenomenal."

Well, I was skeptical, but it sounded damn good. So I went down to the office of the postmaster, Mr. Morlin. "What can I do you for, Louvin," he said, looking up at me from some paperwork on his desk. He was a big, fat bastard, and you could tell he was irritated by having to interrupt his paperwork.

"Mr. Morlin, I've got something that I have to try, and I'd like an extension on my job," I said. "I don't know if it'll work out, but it could be the opportunity of a lifetime."

"Well?" he said. "What is it?"

"My brother and I have a chance to maybe work for WVOK in Alabama. If it works out, it could mean our career."

"It could, could it? How much time would you need?"

"If you can give me a forty-five day extension, that should do it."

He chuckled a little. A real nasty chuckle. "You know your problem, Louvin?" he said. "You need to make up your mind whether you want to be a postal clerk or a hillbilly."

"Does that mean my request's denied?"

"That's exactly what it means," he said. "Request denied."

"Then I'll tell you what you can do with your damn job," I said. "You can stick it where the sun don't shine. I'm finished." And I walked out.

We started recording again for Capitol Records, too. And instead of Fred Rose managing the sessions, Ken Nelson himself flew in from Los Angeles. My time in Korea seemed to have given him some time to think about what he wanted to do with us, and he took over as our A&R man. Ken Nelson was an incredible help to our career. Of course, he was also the one man who probably ruined us, but that was later on.

Ken wasn't very impressive to look at. He wore these thick, black glasses, and his hair was thinning and always kind of mussed up, like he couldn't keep it straight. But he never seemed to get upset about anything, and his voice told you that he was the last word.

Part of what made Ken so special was that he figured out Ira real quick. For Ira, everything had to be just perfect when he recorded. The way we were used to doing it, we'd show up to record a song having already learned it inside and out, so Ira didn't really have much to get upset about. But when we started recording for Capitol and were doing songs that Ken Nelson had chosen, we weren't always prepared. And that meant Ira would just throw a fit if he didn't think one of the songs was up to snuff.

He was a perfectionist. He couldn't understand that there are no such things as perfect people on this earth. There's only ever been one, and as I recall he didn't make out too good in the end. Ira was never satisfied with the job he did in the studio. Or the job I did, for that matter. He could always find mistakes. "Do it again, do it again," he'd say, until you just couldn't stand the sound of his voice.

At first, Ira wouldn't listen to Ken. Ken would tell us that the last version of a song was a take, and Ira'd order us to keep playing it until it sounded like he wanted it to. Or until he just gave up. What I never could get him to understand was that if you keep recording the same tune over and over because you think you can do it a little better, it'll start going the other way, straight downhill.

One day in the studio, we just could not play this one song to Ira's satisfaction. It was just take after take, with Ira saying, "No, that's still wrong. We can do that better."

Finally, on the twenty-sixth take, Ken said, "That's it. I'm keeping take number two, and the other twenty-five I'm throwing away."

But he didn't throw them all away. He kept the twenty-sixth take, and he put it on the album along with the second take. Then, when the album came out, he called us into the studio and said, "I want you to listen to this, Ira."

"Hear what?" Ira said.

"This is your new album. You remember that one song you made us play twenty-six times?"

Ira's face went sullen. "We never did get it right," he said, in his brooding voice.

"Sure," Ken said. "But I want you to listen to this. This is the twenty-sixth take."

We listened to it, and it was obvious that it wasn't very good.

"We just couldn't get it," Ira said, miserably.

"Hold on just one minute," Ken said. And then he played take number two. And there was no denying it. It was twice as good as the twenty-sixth take.

Well, Ira didn't say anything about it, but he did start listening to Ken after that. And you could tell he started to trust him to know what a song needed. I don't think there was ever anyone else in Nashville that Ira trusted on that subject, actually. But he trusted Ken.

And that lesson did help him some. He slid a little on trying to be perfect. Not too far, but a little. After that, when Ken said, "That's a take, what's the next song?" Ira would leave it alone. But if there hadn't been Ken Nelson there to say that with a little authority, there's no telling how long Ira might spend on a song.

Me, I don't use that word, perfect. I never have, at least not in the studio. I have several parts of my life that I would love to make perfect, but singing is not one of them. Every time I step to the microphone, I do the best I can, and once I get through it, I say, "Well, that's as good as I can do it. And if it's not good enough, you can delete it from the session."

Maybe that comes from all those hours spent in the studio with Ira. With him saying, "Do it again," until the sound of his voice was like being touched with the point of a knife. He probably ruined me on trying to be perfect for anybody else, because I got so sick of trying to be perfect for him. It was something you could never tell him, but there was an awful lot of Papa in him. Lord, he could ride you hard. It'd make you frustrated enough to cry.

CHAPTER 27

THE
BLUFF

Moving to Birmingham turned out to be the worst mistake we ever made, just like I'd told Ira it would be. First, the radio job fell through, and then we just couldn't find anywhere to play. This other duet had been working the area for years, and they sung every song we ever wrote. They sounded just like us, and, boy, were they quick. If we had a song come out at ten o'clock in the morning, they'd be singing it on their twelve o'clock show on WVOK. That's how quick they'd learn it. Half the folks out yonder in Birmingham actually thought we were impersonating them when we played a show.

We still weren't making no headway at the Opry, either, and we were getting desperate. Not only had it been our dream since we were kids, we knew if we could get to Nashville we could play the United States from a central point. We were both sick to death of what we'd been doing. Working a radio station for a few months, playing all the decent places we could find around there, and then, when we'd played 'em all, moving on to find another radio station.

We kept auditioning for Jim Denny in the tool shed, and he kept giving us that old "don't call us, we'll call you" shit. And, of course, the call never came. We had no idea what we were doing wrong. We were pretty sure we were as good as anything on the Opry, but we just couldn't get past Denny to save our lives.

Things were really getting rough. When I got back from Korea, I found that Betty, bless her heart, hadn't used up none of the money from my royalties, nor from my Army paycheck, and it all added up to about ten thousand dollars. But even with the car paid for, we'd used almost all of it by the time Birmingham played out. We were all living together in a two-room duplex, slowly starving to death.

Finally, I couldn't take anymore. I told Ira, "We gotta shit or get off the pot."

"What pot?" he said. We were sitting in the kitchen, drinking coffee. "There ain't no pot. There's nothing we can try that we haven't tried already."

"Then I vote that we quit," I said. "I'm sure I can get my job back at the Post Office, whether or not Morlin likes it. When I turn sixty-five, I can sit on the creek bank and drown worms. We'll never get any kind of retirement out of this, we can't get nothing going."

"For once, I agree with you," he said.

"All right," I said. "Well, before we agree, let's make a deal. I wanna try one more thing."

"What's that?"

"I wanna call Ken Nelson and see if he can get us on the Opry. We're crazy, man. We can't do everything ourselves. I'll make one more call, and if it don't work out, we'll go our separate ways."

"Ken Nelson ain't gonna do shit," said Ira. "There ain't nothing he can do."

Well, I couldn't predict whether that was true or not, but I didn't see any sense in not trying. So I went out and walked up the street until I found a payphone, and I called Ken Nelson. I told him how low we were in Birmingham, and that we were thinking about giving up. "I'm not bullshitting you, Ken," I said. "If we can't make Nashville, we're just gonna quit."

"Why don't you let me see what I can do?" he said.

"That's what I was hoping you'd say. Do you know anybody on the Opry?"

"Well, I know Jack Stapp pretty well."

"Who's Jack Stapp?" I asked.

Ken laughed a little. "He's the boss over there. I thought you told me you were auditioning?"

"We were," I said. "We were told the boss was Jim Denny. That's who we've been playing for."

This time he laughed a lot. "Jim Denny," he repeated. "Jim Denny's the damn stage manager. He doesn't have anything to do with who plays on the Opry."

Well, I didn't know what to say to that. I'd probably have been madder'n hell if I'd had the time to think about it, but I didn't really have time.

"I'll tell you what," he said. "Give me your phone number, and I'll call you back in a few minutes."

"I don't have a phone number," I said, "They shut our phone off last week. I'm at a payphone."

"Then give me the number of the payphone, and guard the damn thing so nobody gets on it," he said. "I'll call Jack Stapp and get right back with you."

I'll tell you what, I would have killed anyone that tried to tie up that phone. I guarded it like my life depended on it. Which, in a way, it did. But sure enough, he called back in less than twenty minutes, just like he promised.

"Well?" I said.

"It went like this," he said. "I told Jack that I had a duet on my label that I'd like to have on the Grand Ole Opry. But if he didn't want them he should let me know right away, because the Ozark Jubilee did."

That was pretty smart on Ken's part. The Opry was afraid of the Ozark Jubilee, because they had the first television network show. Red Foley had already left, and so had Porter Wagoner and Pee Wee King and six or eight other of the Opry members. So Jack told Ken, "Now, waitaminute, Ken, we don't need nobody else going to Springfield. Okay, tell 'em they're on this coming Friday."

I could scarcely believe it when Ken gave me that message. But he was a man you could trust, he didn't bullshit you. I ran right back to the house with so many bubbles in my throat that I could barely breathe. "Ken Nelson says we're on the Opry starting this Friday night," I managed to blurt out. Not many things could leave Ira speechless, but that did. At least until he started whooping.

After we'd calmed down enough we could make sense, we packed up Betty and Sonny and sent them off in the Studebaker to Memphis where Betty's folks lived, and did the same with Ira's wife, Bobbie Lowery, sending her in Ira's old car to Knoxville. Ira and I had no doubt that it wouldn't be a month before we became millionaires now that we were on the Opry. "We'll see you girls before you know it," we told 'em. And then Ira and I caught a Trailways bus and rode to Nashville.

And that's how we got on the Opry. Purely by a bluff. A flat-out lie. And I've been a member ever since.

CHAPTER 28

THE OPRY

At the time we started on the Opry, they had two versions. There was the Grand Ole Opry, which was held on Saturday night at the Ryman where we'd been auditioning, and then there was the Friday Night Opry where we'd be playing, and that was held at Seventh and Union, in the offices of the National Life & Accident Insurance Company building. That was also where all the Opry offices were, so that's where Ira and I went when we arrived in Nashville.

Neither of us talked much as we walked over from the bus station, carrying our suitcases. It had taken us from 1941 to 1955 for our dream to come true, and we hadn't really ever thought it was that big a dream. Even when we were kids singing under the bed in our living room we thought for sure that if we could just get somebody to listen then we'd be able to get to the Opry, no problem.

Well, that's not quite how it happened. Everything worked out, but awful slowly. We weren't working on our schedule, we were working on somebody else's schedule. Like it or not, we couldn't rush it, and we couldn't drag it. We just had to take it as it came, and be ready for whatever got thrown at us. I'll tell you this, though, I wouldn't want to wish our path on anybody. To try for something for as long as we did and then make it through on a bluff.

Of course, we were incredibly nervous when we walked into that building. We gave our names to the receptionist, and she took us office to office, meeting everybody. First Jack Stapp, then Vito Pellettieri, the stage manager for the Friday show, and then the radio announcer, David Cobb. The place was a madhouse. People running from office to office, secretaries shuffling around, musicians tuning their instruments. It was a bunch of shit we didn't really need, to be honest, but the protocol was that we had to meet everybody, so we did.

And then, wouldn't you know it, the last office we went into was Jim Denny's, the guy who'd kept rejecting our auditions. And he was not having a good day.

It turned out that he had a publishing company, and the way he worked it was that if you didn't record his songs, you didn't get any dates on the Opry. He couldn't make anyone a member, but as soon as you got on there, he was the one who decided when you got scheduled. Well, it was a monopoly, and they were finally breaking it up that very day. They'd told him he'd have to get rid of his publishing company or leave, and he thought they couldn't fire him because he did too many things. Well, they did fire his ass, but first he called all his cronies and tried to talk them into leaving with him.

That's what he was doing when we walked into his office and sat down. He was sitting at his desk, making his phone calls. He was in his three-piece suit and hat, and he'd pick up the phone and say, "Mary Claire, get me Carl Smith." And then they'd talk for three or four minutes and he'd hang up, and it'd be, "Mary Claire, get me Minnie Pearl." He was acting as if we wasn't even in the room. "Mary Claire, get me Hank Snow." "Mary Claire, get me Webb Pierce." "Jimmy Dickens." All the people that he thought he could talk into leaving.

Ira always had a shorter fuse than I did. I don't know if it was to his advantage or not, but finally he got tired of waiting, and he stood up and said, "Well, Mr. Denny, we'll see you tonight on the Friday Night Opry."

Denny stopped talking on the phone. He pulled his glasses down his long nose, and looked straight over them at Ira. Then he covered the receiver of the phone and said to us, "Boys, you're in high timber, you better shit and git it."

"Well, Mr. Denny," Ira said, "we've got the saws, you just show us where the woods are."

We never did get along with Denny very good after that. He pegged us as smart-asses. I don't think he was used to getting broadsided by a good joke. The way I always figured him, he liked his artists best when they were kissing his ass. And most of them did.

After Denny, we were through until the show. And it occurred to us that we didn't have anywhere to stay. Luckily, we ran into a few pickers that'd heard of us, and they told us that when most folks come into Nashville like we did, as stragglers, they stayed at Ma Boscobel's. She lived over in East Nashville, on Boscobel Street as it turned out, and she was known for being cheap. She sure was. It wasn't the worst place I ever lived, I guess. But it was bad enough that they had a day shift and a night shift that slept on the same bed. She was getting all the boarders in there that she could get.

We knew that in the Ryman two dressing rooms split off the stage, a woman's restroom and changing room, and on the other side, a little aisle for the men that had a urinal and nothing else. We didn't know what the National Life & Accident Insurance Company building had, but we figured it couldn't hurt to be ready. So we got dressed and tuned our instruments in our room before walking back down to the building.

They had a little backstage area behind the curtain where you waited, and it had the program posted so you could see who you was gonna follow. Well, when we got up there, all of a sudden my pant leg started a'shaking, and I swear my vision just dimmed out. It was as if all the air in the room had been sucked out. I couldn't breathe at all. And then, just like that first time we sang at the Haynes reunion for Mama, everything seemed to focus in on Ira, and he was standing there grinning, just as confident as could be. "You ready?" he said.

I did the best I could to grin back at him. "I believe I am," I said.

The icing on the cake was that Roy Acuff gave us our introduction as new members. We didn't know that was gonna happen, and when we saw him getting up there to do it, I was scared I wouldn't be able to sing, I got so choked up. That memory of standing outside our schoolhouse watching him perform, measuring ourselves against him and dreaming of singing on the Opry, almost overcame me entirely. "Ladies and gentlemen, the newest members of the Opry, the Louvin Brothers," Acuff said. "They'll be here a long time, and I'm gonna let 'em show you why."

Then we stepped out onstage, and my freaking legs turned to rubber again. I truly did good to stand up. But I kept my eyes on Ira, and once we started into our first song, "Love Thy Neighbor As Thyself," I was fine. And the crowd even liked us enough that they gave us an encore.

The next night at the Ryman was even better. This time I wasn't nearly as nervous, and we played two shows, doing two songs on each show. And after that show, we were met by a guy that wanted to book us, and that was a real blessing. We'd never had a real booker before. I'd always just handled all the mail and bookings myself.

Singing on the Opry

It just kept rolling, getting better and better. It was only a couple months before we had enough money to send for the girls. I found a place for Betty and me with one bedroom, a living room, and a bath. I figured we didn't need much, because you can always put a young kid in a playpen and let him sleep there. That's what I thought, but it wasn't too long before we needed a larger place.

Our booker kept us busy, though, so I can't say I enjoyed much of our new home. I was on the road all the time, and Betty had to care of the children. Get 'em in school, and do everything by herself that a Mama and Papa's supposed to do together.

But that's the way it is in the music business. You have to decide which one you want to do the worst. Do you wanna be in the music business, or do you wanna stay home and take care of the kids? And that's not a hard decision to make for a picker.

I just did what I could with Betty and the kids, making the most of what few times we did get together at home. And Ira and I worked so that the girls always had enough money to keep grub in the house and the lights on. I think I withheld ten dollars a day for food and cigarettes, and gave Betty everything else.

Betty and me

CHAPTER 29

WHEN I STOP DREAMING

The problem we kept running into after joining the Opry was that we were a gospel-only duet. That's what we signed on to Capitol as and that's all the records they would let us put out. It made it incredibly hard to make a living playing shows. We just couldn't seem to find the right audience. The gospel folks didn't want us around because they considered us carnival people. They all played pianos and looked down on us who played stringed instruments. On the flip side, we weren't really welcome at the country music venues because we would quiet down the audience too much. Our gospel music made everybody feel guilty that they were there having a good time. We was pretty close to being a fart in a whirlwind.

Finally, we couldn't take it anymore. And the next time we were in the studio with Ken Nelson, Ira spoke up. "So, Ken," he said. "What would you think if we was to record a secular song or two?"

Ken just looked at him.

"Nothing that might get us in trouble," Ira continued quickly.

"Oh shit," Ken said, "You're trying to pull a Martha Carson."

That was exactly what we had hoped he wouldn't say. See, Martha Carson was this gospel artist who'd tried to go secular just a couple months before. Her husband, Xavier Cosse, had convinced her to do a heavier kind of music, and drop her neckline down to a secular height. She'd managed to do nothing but piss off all her gospel fans and get thrown off the label.

"We're not gonna sing any risqué music," Ira said. "We're gonna sing music that grandma and the kids could listen to together and not be insulted by."

"It's your career," Ken said, though he didn't look too excited. "But if it don't catch on with the public, I expect you'll be gone just like Martha Carson. And there won't be nothing I can do about it."

"We'll take that chance," Ira said. "We have to take that chance. We can't make a living doing only gospel."

There was this one song that Ira had been working on all the way back to when I was in Korea. It was called "When I Stop Dreaming" and we figured it was the strongest secular song we had. Both Ira and I loved that song. We were each dreamers in our own way. Everybody is. The doers make their dreams happen, but everybody knows what it's like to dream.

I'll tell you, though, we were nervous when we walked in the studio with Ken Nelson to record it. Even Ira couldn't stop fidgeting with his hands. And Ken was just as scared as we were, I think. He even brought his own song for us to try in hopes it would hit if ours didn't. It was called "Pitfall," and the damn thing nearly drove us bowlegged and blind trying to get it down. Neither Ira nor I had ever played it before, and we ended up with something like twenty takes before we got done with it. Besides those two songs, we also recorded "Alabama" again, which seemed like a safe bet, and then a

Jimmy Rule song that we'd been rehearsing for some time called "Memories And Tears."

But Ira and I were right to pin our hopes where we did. "When I Stop Dreaming" hit big. It was our first single after we joined the Opry, and it made it into the top ten on *Billboard*. It had the staying power we'd hoped for, too, and was recorded by everybody from Johnny Cash to Ray Charles at one time or another.

All of a sudden, we were making real money. So the first thing we did was to buy ourselves two Nudie suits each. One white with gold leaves, and one black with gold leaves. Everybody wore 'em. Elvis, Johnny Cash, Hank Williams. Even later, the first thing Gram Parsons did when he got a record contract was to run out and buy one. A Nudie suit was almost like a uniform for a country star.

Ira and me in our new Nudie suits

My black suit is in the Country Music Hall of Fame in Nashville, but I don't know what the hell happened to the white one. I know Ira gave both of his away. He hated them, and he never would hang on to anything. That's part of why they never had nothing much in the museums to represent the Louvin Brothers. After forty-five years, there ain't much left except what's in my head.

I can't really blame Ira for hating them, though. My Lord, they were hot. If you put one on when you had to perform in an auditorium where they didn't have air-conditioning, the suit would weigh a couple hundred pounds by the time you got through with a show. You had to hang it in the car by the window where it could get air, and maybe a couple days later it would finally dry out. If you didn't have a show in between, that is.

We didn't wear them long. As soon as they wore out enough that we could justify hanging 'em up, we went back to wearing casual slacks, sport coats, and a nice pair of boots. We never got too much into clothing, even when we got more successful. The outfits we wore might not even have been alike. Ira and I had totally different taste in clothes, so when he went and bought his, I'd go to the same place, but I'd usually end up with something that was kind of oddball up against what he bought. A few like Little Jimmy Dickens, Porter Wagoner, and Bill Anderson would wear the real loud clothing, but we always wore the kind of toned-down outfit that you could have gone to a funeral in and not stuck out as a yokum.

It served us well, I guess. Might have been better for our career if we could have continued the Nudie stuff, but that shit cost like three thousand dollars for just a coat and pants, and our budget would have been mightily strained if we had to add a couple of them a year. Of course, they're deductible, but before you can deduct 'em from your taxes, you have to deduct 'em from your salary.

The biggest change that came as a result of us finally making some money was that Ira could finally afford to divorce Bobbie. Somehow, he just couldn't seem to keep a wife, even when he was too broke to really screw up. And once we had money to spend, he was able to indulge some of those habits that maybe it would've been better for him to be too broke to mess around with.

Of course, Bobbie took him to the fucking cleaners. In this world, you can get as much justice as you can afford, and if you can't afford much justice, you won't get much. And even with the money we were making, Ira was always broke from spending it on girls and booze. It being Ira, though, he didn't bother fighting Bobbie on the child support. That would have been too practical. He just didn't pay it.

That came to a head one night when we were getting ready to go on the Opry, and I looked over and saw two cops standing there by the stage.

"Can I help you?" I asked one of 'em.

"You Ira Louvin?" the cop asked me.

"I'm Charlie Louvin, his brother," I said. "What the shit's he done now?"

"He's behind on his child support," the cop said, and showed me the paperwork. Sure enough, he was about four hundred and fifty dollars behind, and they'd added a penalty on top of it.

Well, I had just opened my mouth to say that he wasn't in the building, when here come Ira up onstage. "What do these germs want?"

That was that. They hauled his ass off to jail until I could round up enough money to get his debts paid off.

That wasn't the last time it happened, either. It got to the point where the cops were waiting on us about every three to four months. In fact, that was the only time Ira would pay his child support.

What saved us was that our booker Preston Temple and

I had put together a songbook we sold on the road. I don't think Ira even knew about it, let alone how much money it made. Preston just took the cash home and put it in a little lockbox, and then, whenever Ira was arrested, Preston would go home and count up enough to pay his way out of jail.

A lot of the money was in spare change, because that's how people paid us. So there were times that the police would want to know where Preston and I got the money. Sometimes they would actually hold us until they checked around to see if any pinball machines in the area had been robbed. But we got Ira out of it every time. And, it being Ira, it never did seem to bother him to step right back in it.

He had the money, too. He just spent it on other things. He was neglectful, is all. Neglectful and completely lacking in common sense. Preston and I never got us a penny out of those songbooks, not one. But it got Ira out of jail a dozen times, so I guess it was worth it.

CHAPTER 30

TROUBLE

We'd only been on the Opry a couple months, when out of nowhere we got a call to come into Roy Acuff's office. Neither Ira nor I had really had a chance to talk to Roy Acuff yet. He'd say hello now and then, and he'd given us that great introduction our first night on the Opry, but we hadn't heard much from him since. All kinds of things went through our heads. Maybe he'd tell us what an honor it was to have us on the Opry, or how much he'd enjoyed our last show. Maybe he'd heard the story about how we'd gone to see him as kids, and wanted to talk to us about it. We didn't know, but we walked up to his office feeling pretty good about ourselves for getting noticed.

Then Roy Acuff's boss opened the door. And we saw his boss behind him. And pretty much everybody else's boss, too. I felt my heart cork itself in my throat. Acuff was very important at the Opry, one of the biggest single shareholders in the

National Life & Accident Insurance Company, and I'd been bawled out enough in my life to know what it looked like.

He was sitting behind his desk, just looking at us. "Boys," he said, by way of greeting. He was fidgeting. That was the thing about Acuff, he really couldn't stand conflict of any kind. He just wasn't built for it. He had this crazy, curly hair, a big grin for everybody, and he just wasn't no good at coming down on people.

"Hello Mr. Acuff," I said. "What can we do for you?"

"Let me see if I can tell the story, Roy," Acuff's boss said, and Acuff nodded. "It goes like this, boys. We heard from Brother Oswald that y'all were running around saying Roy Acuff here is bad for the country music business. Is there anything to it?"

"Man, I've got no idea what you're talking about," Ira said.

"It was one of your shows in Virginia," Acuff's boss said. "Oswald said he heard it straight from the manager of the place you played there."

"Oh, shit," Ira said. "That guy," and both he and I knew what they were talking about immediately.

It was this show date down on the edge of Virginia, just a little northeast of Knoxville, Tennessee. We'd pulled up there on a rainy afternoon, and there were all kinds of things going wrong. It was run poorly, the sound setup was a joke, but probably the worst thing was that it hadn't been advertised good at all, so barely anybody showed up.

At the end of the night, after everybody had left and we were loading all our gear back into the car in the rain, the manager of the venue came to us, holding a paper sack.

"What's that?" I asked.

"It's your pay," the guy said.

I took it from him and opened it up. There was only three hundred dollars in the bag. "Mister," I said, "We didn't come here for the door. We came for a flat rate. If you've forgotten that, you might wanna get your contract out."

He sort of shuffled around for a minute, and then said, "Well, three or four months ago Roy Acuff was up here and he didn't have a very good crowd, so he wouldn't take any of the money. He gave it all back."

"That's great," I said. "Mr. Acuff's got the millions that he can work for nothing if he wants to. We're depending on this work out here to make a living, and we can't afford to."

After some more hemming and hawing, he paid us the agreed price and we left. But somehow the conversation got back to Brother Oswald, only all switched around in a way that didn't even resemble what we'd said. In fact, it might've been an example of what goes around comes around, in that we almost got kicked off the Opry the same way we got on, through a lie.

Anyway, Acuff's boss did most of the talking. He told us exactly what he'd heard we said, that Acuff was bad for the

Roy Acuff and me

business, that he was ruining it for the rest of us working musicians. When he got done I looked over at Ira to see if he wanted to answer. But I could tell by the look on his face that I'd better handle this one if I wanted to keep our spot on the Opry. So I jumped in just as quick as I could. "That ain't nothing like what happened," I said.

"Is Brother Oswald lying?" Acuff's boss said.

"I didn't say that," I said. "Brother Oswald might've heard that from the guy up there, but that ain't how it was."

"Then how was it?" Acuff's boss said.

"Well, for one thing, I didn't say that Acuff was bad for the business. I just said that Roy Acuff could afford to not get paid for a show, but we couldn't."

"Is there any way you can prove it?" Acuff's boss asked. I was sick down to my boots. This was definitely not the way I'd thought our first real meeting with Roy Acuff would go, that's for sure. Here was the man who'd inspired us to be here, and he was accusing us of running him down. I couldn't take being called a liar, neither. "Is that what this is?" I asked. "Whether or not we remain members of the Opry depends on us proving something you know we can't prove?"

"It might," Acuff's boss said.

"Well, I told you what happened," I said, "and I don't care what anybody says. If us being members of the Grand Ole Opry depends on nothing but whether or not Roy Acuff likes us, then we'll leave now."

Roy slid in at that point. "No, no," he said. "Let's not get ridiculous here. Maybe Oswald did hear it wrong. Sometimes he does that."

With that said, it finally started to cool down. But it had got to the smoking point, where any statement you made you'd have to live up to. That story got spread around some, too, and most people got it wrong. It's bad when there's only three or four people around when something like that happens. Especially when two of 'em die, and one of 'em tells some big cock and bull story about something bad you did. You know it's a lie, and the person telling it knows it's a lie, but you can't really prove it. It's just his word against yours. But that's the way it's always been. You can be misrepresented, and it's so easy it'll make your head swim.

But, by God, I never would say anything like that about Acuff. He was the Opry. Everybody knew that when Mr. Acuff passed away, the Opry would change. And it has. It's like upside down from what it was when Acuff was living. It's gone to hell in a hand basket.

CHAPTER 31

ELVIS

By 1956, we had a few hits under our belt. There was "When I Stop Dreaming" and then "I Don't Believe You've Met My Baby," which was even bigger. We were as hot an act as they had on the Opry, and one day we got a call from Colonel Tom Parker to ask us if we wanted to tour with Elvis. Elvis hadn't become a phenomenon yet, but Parker knew he could if he could just get people, to see him play. Once you get a true entertainer in front of people, they can entertain 'em. But you have to find a way to get the people seated first. If he'd have put Elvis' name up in lights, there might not be five people in the audience. So we were used to fill the seats, along with the Carter Family, Justin Tubb, and Benny Martin.

Elvis Presley was a true, honest-to-God Louvin Brothers fan, and so was his mother. Every time we'd have a new gospel record out, Betty and I would swing by the Presley's house out there on Audubon Drive. Elvis never was there, the Colonel kept him pretty busy making his gambling money, but Mrs. Presley was always home, and we'd give the record to her. She was always cordial, and I think she really appreciated that we brought her the albums. Maybe that's why Elvis said that the Louvin Brothers were his all-time favorite duet.

I'll admit that I thought he was a fad. That he'd just caught on with a song or two, and probably wouldn't ever have another hit. But then there was this one time when Betty and I went to his home in Memphis to drop off one of our gospel albums for his mother, and I seen this middle-aged woman out there, down on her knees and reaching up under the wooden rail fence to pull grass. Just so she could take it home and say, "I took this from Elvis Presley's yard." And then I knew Elvis was no fad. He was loved by the old and the young, and everybody in between. He was simply a hit walking around just hunting for a place to happen. It took Chet Atkins' and Colonel Tom's help, but it did happen.

The funny thing was, after Elvis left Sun Records, it took Atkins and Parker six weeks in the studio to get the sound that Elvis had at Sun Records. They was trying everything they could to re-create it, but unlike Sun Records, they had real expensive equipment, and they couldn't get it right for the longest time. When they finally did find the magic button, that was it, though. I know two or three people that wrote songs Elvis recorded, and if that's all the money they had coming in, they could still make a living.

It didn't take us long to figure out what kind of man Colonel Tom Parker was on that tour. Mostly, we were scheduled in school auditoriums, and usually there were enough people there for a second show when we finished the first one. So Colonel Tom got in the habit of sending his gopher back to tell us in the dressing room that the next show would start in fifteen minutes, as soon as he could get the people in. And that we were expected to play it for free. Colonel Tom never tried to deal with the artists directly if he could help it. He always used a gopher. I always figured that was because he knew he was a fourteen-carat asshole, and that his being in front of an artist would likely cause an argument that would cost him money.

Anyway, after a few nights, everybody'd had about enough of doing two shows and only being paid for one. After all, the only person making any money on that second show was Colonel Tom Parker. So we all got together and decided to make a complaint. And we chose Ira as the one to deliver the complaint to Colonel Tom Parker's gopher.

So when the gopher came back the following night and told us that the next show started in fifteen minutes, Ira told him, "You tell Colonel Tom, if he wants to do a second show, he can come on back here with something green in his hand."

Well, the kid knew what that meant. But when Colonel Tom came back to see us, he didn't have anything green in his hand. Instead, he had a bunch of excuses. "I was gonna give everybody a bonus at the end of the tour," he whined. Which was bullshit, of course. He even bellyached to Justin Tubb. "Justin, you know I wouldn't try to screw you. I bought you your first pony when you was only a child."

He just had no shame. But it worked. Justin nodded. "Yessir, I remember that, Mr. Parker," and after Justin went, everybody started caving in. It began to look like Ira was the only one who had a problem playing two shows. But after that, if Parker advertised one show, we only did one show. I'm telling you, the man would turn down five thousand people standing out in the front yard just to keep from paying the artists for the work they did. That was the kind of man he was.

He was a potbellied pig. That's the best way to describe him. Maybe ten inches too much fat around the gut and a couple more hanging off his chin, just flabby all over. But he was a marketing genius along the lines of Smilin' Eddie Hill.

One of the biggest shows we played on the Elvis tour was in an outside ball stadium. I doubt anyone who was there at that show would ever forget it, because at the end Elvis collapsed onstage. Fainted dead away, like with heat exhaustion. Lucky for him there was an ambulance waiting only ten feet from the stage.

Well, back at the hotel, they'd been nice enough to hold the grill open so we could get short orders, and we were in the bar area laughing and shooting the shit when Elvis walked in after his ambulance ride. He ordered a cup of coffee and sat down with us.

"What happened to you out there?" I asked him.

"Aw, the Colonel put me up to that," he said. "The ambulance circled around a couple of times and then brought me straight back here."

"What'd he have you do that for?"

"He said it'd make the next show a big deal, but I don't see how." He smiled a little bit. "I told him I didn't want to break my guitar falling on it like that, but he told me he'd buy me a dozen guitars if it worked."

Well, there was a television in the bar, and right then somebody called out, "Look at that, Elvis, you're on TV."

Sure enough, there he was in his red sport coat, being loaded in the ambulance. And the announcer was saying they'd be updating fans all night on Elvis' condition, but it was expected he'd be just fine for the next night's show. We switched around the channels, and on all three networks, it was the same thing. That's how clever Parker was. He couldn't have bought Elvis that kind of publicity for a million bucks.

That tour was when he really caught on. Before that, nobody really knew what to do with him. I mean, he did some pretty wild stuff onstage, shaking around inside his clothes, and at first the audience didn't even know what he was doing. But the youth sure caught on, and before that tour was over, he was as hot as anybody in the United States.

Later, Elvis learned that there was a lot about Parker he didn't know. He was an illegal alien, for one thing. He came over from Holland, slid into Tampa, and created his own job to support himself. He walked down to the city offices and told the clerk he wanted to apply for the job of city dog-catcher. Well, she just looked at him funny and said, "We don't need a dogcatcher, sir. We don't have a dog problem."

So Parker got in his pickup truck, got himself a cage, and went out and picked up a load of the mangiest, ugliest dogs he could find, drove 'em to the best part of town, and turned 'em out. In a few days, all these uppity people in Tampa were calling the city to say that all these ugly strays were out here and somebody needs to do something. And sure enough, when Parker went back and applied for the job again, she hired him.

I don't know how he got hooked in with managing, but he managed a lot of people before he found Elvis. Eddy Arnold, Hank Snow, and Ernest Tubb, being three of them, and there were no country singers much bigger than them. Once he became your manager, he owned you, too. At least that's how he felt about it. Elvis' family had to sue him to get him to quit drawing money on Elvis after he died. Parker had been drawing his percentage, which was something like fifty percent, for a year after Elvis passed.

He was a big-time gambler, too. If he had fifty thousand dollars at nine o'clock at night, it'd be gone by midnight. He actually rented a place on the top floor of one of the biggest casinos in Vegas. That way, every time his money would come in from Elvis, all he had to do was get on the elevator for a few seconds to make it to the middle of the gambling district. He died broke, of course.

Unfortunately, Ira had one other run-in with Elvis and Colonel Parker on that tour. And the second one was a little more personal. See, Elvis closed every show, so when he'd get to the dressing room, we'd all be back there already sitting around. And this one time he came back, sat down at this old piano that was there, and started playing some old gospel song. When he finished the song, he spun around on the stool and said to everybody, "You know, that's the music I really love."

Well, Ira'd been drinking some. It was happening more and more by that time, now that we'd started to have a little success. "Well, you damn white nigger," he said to Elvis. "Why do you play that crap on the stage if that's what you love?"

Elvis just grinned at him. It wasn't the first time he'd been called a white nigger, I'm sure. A lot of people in Nashville felt the same way. "When I'm out there, I try to do what they want to hear," he said, easily. "When I'm back here, I can do what I want."

Elvis Presley

That was the end of it. And, if you think about it, what Elvis said made perfect sense. But, of course, a bunch of people
spread it around that there was a big fistfight, and Ira had
to be dragged off from trying to choke him. There was no
punching or choking, though. People just added that in because it made things a little juicier.

Still, we never worked another date with Elvis after that
tour. And Elvis never recorded a single Louvin Brothers
song, even though he said we were his favorite duet, and we
were known to be his Mama's favorite gospel singers. He recorded half a dozen Hank Williams songs, several Don Gibson songs, various other Acuff-Rose artists, but he never cut
a Louvin Brothers song. Not one.

If I had to guess, I'd say that one statement by Ira cost the
Louvin Brothers music catalog two or three million dollars.
And I don't believe Elvis took offense, either. It was a stupid
thing to say, but everybody knew how Ira was. I figure somebody had to have told Colonel Parker about it. Elvis Presley
didn't hold a grudge, he was a good boy. But Parker sure as
hell did. And he controlled everything Elvis did and didn't
record.

I never saw Elvis after that tour, neither, though I did try
once. I was working Memphis, and Elvis' stepmother was at
my show. Well, my boy Sonny was with me, and he wanted to
meet Elvis, so I went up to Elvis' stepmother after I got done
playing and asked her if he was around. "Well, he's right over
at the house," she said. "Why don't you just go on out there
and meet him right now?"

I had a little time before my second show, and it was only
four or five miles out to the house, so we got in the car and
drove out. But when we got inside, the only person we found
was Elvis' father. Elvis himself was sleeping. So I stood
around talking to his father for a while hoping he'd wake up,
and after about thirty or forty minutes, I finally asked, "What
time does Elvis get out of bed?"

"Whenever he wakes up," his father said.

"Could you go on up and tell him I'm here?" I asked. "If he didn't want to come down, that's fine, but I'd like for him to know that I'm here and would like to see him."

His father just laughed. "I can't go up there."

"What do you mean you can't go up there?" I said. "You're his father."

"There's two guards between here and Elvis' door," he said, "They'd turn me right around."

Boy, this is wild, I thought. I'm probably twelve feet from the window to Elvis' room, and I'd have to go through two guards to get to him. Maybe I oughta get some small pebbles and throw 'em up against his window-glass.

I didn't, though. And we never did get to see him. We stayed as long as we could, but I had to get back for my second show. Of course, I doubt he would have looked forward to seeing Ira again, but he and I had always got along. I was just trying to get him out where I could shake his hand and maybe get a picture with him and my kid, but it didn't turn out that way.

It wasn't too long after that when he died. Which I expected to happen, of course. Elvis said all the time that he'd never live to be a day older than his mother was when she died. He was a real mama's boy, and, of course, if he had lived one more day he would have been older than she was.

I've always believed he done it on purpose. That he snuffed himself. There wasn't nobody, even doctors, that knew anything more about dope than Elvis did. You can't convince me he accidentally killed himself that way. He knew exactly what you could mix and what you could not mix. He'd been managing it a good many years.

CHAPTER 32

TOURING
WITH
PAPA

Papa was very proud of us, I have no doubt about that. He wasn't the kind of man you could expect to do a lot gushing over you or anything like that, but nobody tracked our career any closer than he did. He even bought a radio and put it in the living room so he could listen to us on the Opry. And he tuned in every night we played.

A couple times, we even managed to get him up on the Opry with us, playing his banjo. He loved it, of course, being up there onstage. Before he'd come out to Nashville, he'd call everybody he knew to tell them that he was gonna be on the Opry. And then, as quick as he got home the following day, he'd call all the same people to see if they listened. Finally, I had to tell him, "Shit, Papa, being on the Opry's costing you three hundred dollars in long distance phone calls every time. You just can't afford it."

But for all that he was proud of us, you could tell he still didn't think much of what we did as far as it being a job.

Singing on the Opry stage

Surely not compared to the work he did out in the fields. To him, it just looked like we were spending our lives playing around. "When are you boys gonna quit traipsing around all over the country and get you a real job?" he'd ask every time we visited him.

It would get on my nerves a little bit, but it pissed Ira off to no end. He'd fume and cuss the whole ride home after one of those comments. He never could take much criticism from Papa at all, and the older he got and the more he drank, the less of it he could take. Finally, I told him one time, "If it pisses you off so much, why don't you do something about it?"

"I believe I will," he said. He was quiet for about fifteen minutes, just looking out the window smoking a cigarette.

And then he started to laugh. "And here's what we're gonna do," he said, and he laid out his plan for me.

Well, we waited until the part of the year we knew Papa was laying by time, when he'd planted all he could plant, and he couldn't get in a crop nor plow no more. And, since we knew he didn't have nothing to do for four or five weeks, we stopped by and conned him into riding to a few shows with us. "Come on, Papa," Ira said. "We'll have a ball. You can bring your banjo and tour the country with us. It'll be just like you're in our band."

Papa couldn't really think of any reason to say no, so he agreed. And Ira and I loaded him and his banjo up in our 1956 Cadillac limo, and started driving down to Miami for our first show. We drove for four or five hours before Papa yawned and said, "So, what time do you boys sleep?"

That Cadillac was pretty close to that air-cooled Franklin that we remembered Acuff riding in, and we were proud of it. "We sleep whenever we get a chance, Papa," Ira said. "You're sitting in the most expensive bed that we could afford."

"Ah," he said. "I can't go to sleep a'riding."

"I'll bet you don't say that the day after tomorrow," Ira said, and winked at me.

We drove on, traveling all night to get to Miami, where we did the first show. And then, knowing we didn't have time to check into a hotel if we wanted to make New Orleans for our second show, we set right back out on the road. If you had a good booker, he'd put you in the places that'd make the most money, and he didn't think nothing about putting them a thousand miles apart. That's what pills were for, after all.

You can make a thousand miles in fifteen hours if you're good. But it's always a race. I can't count the number of times I've shown up with barely time to shave my face in the nearest creek. Put the foam on and shave some in the still water, then rinse out your razor, and when the water's still again, shave some more. Ain't no telling how many times I done it. It might not be as good as warm water, but it's water, anyway.

We got out about two-thirds of the way to New Orleans before Papa spoke up again. "So, boys," he said. "When do you take a bath?"

By way of answer, I angled off the interstate and pulled into this truck stop. Inside, I gave Papa two dollars and said, "Go on over there and give it to the man. Tell him you want to take a shower."

He shook his head. "I ain't taking no shower with a bunch of truckers."

"That's a private shower room, Papa," I said. "It'll be only you."

Ira and I just shook our heads watching him make his way to the shower room. He was walking all hunched over, like he'd been beat with a baseball bat. I was trying not to start laughing out loud, and Ira's eyes were twinkling in a way that was almost scary.

It took him about ten minutes to finish up. And when he come back out he did look a little freshed up, but I knew he hadn't slept since Alabama. "Well," said Ira, slapping the table. "You've had your shower, Papa. It's time we got back out on the road." I thought Papa might start crying there for a second.

We drove through the night, finally making it to New Orleans. And after we got done with New Orleans, I knew we barely had time to make it to Corpus Christi, so we headed straight back out on the road. And here come Papa again. "I don't know how you boys do it," he said. "I sure could use some sleep."

"Just lay your head back and go to sleep, Papa," I said.

"I can't ride in no car and sleep," he said miserably.

By the end of our trip, Papa was so tired he wouldn't even

play the banjo with us. "I believe I'll just leave the banjo in the case," he said on the last show.

"They'll love you, Papa," Ira said, trying not to bust out laughing.

"They'll love you, too," Papa said in a voice that sounded like he was about to die.

When we'd finished all five dates and got back to his house in Alabama, he wasted no time getting out of the car. Nor in informing Ira and I that that's not the way he would like to make a living.

And he never again said, "Why don't you get you a real job?" Because he knew then that we had a real job. It may not have been as hard as digging ditches or some other ways of life, but if you did it right, it was plenty hard.

CHAPTER 33

TRAGIC
SONGS OF
LIFE

The audiences are what brought us to cutting our first full-length Capitol Records album, *Tragic Songs of Life*. From the time we were kids, if anybody asked us to do a song or two, you can bet that one of them would be a murder ballad or a tragic song. We wrote a couple of the songs on that album, but most of them were ones that Ira and I had done from the time we were singing under Papa's high bed.

We did "Mary of the Wild Moor," and another one that may be just as sad called "In the Pines." It's more than a hundred years old, about a guy who spends all night out in the woods, in the pines, where the sun never shines, shivering in the cold, wondering where his woman's gone. In some of the versions, the guy ends up getting his head chopped off by the train his wife leaves on. But in ours, he just mourns her leaving. That was enough for us.

The big one on that album was "Knoxville Girl," which we'd been performing since we were kids. We'd sing it at the drop of a hat, and, hell, if you weren't careful, we might knock the hat out of your hand. In the old country, it was called "The Wexford Girl," and I've heard it goes all the way back to Elizabethan times. It's an exceptionally morbid song, about a man who beats his girlfriend to death. The reason he murders her is never said right up front, but you can figure it out from the lyrics.

> *She fell down on her bended knees,*
> *For mercy she did cry.*
> *Oh, Willie dear, don't kill me here,*
> *I'm unprepared to die.*
> *She never spoke another word,*
> *I only beat her more.*
> *Until the ground around me,*
> *Within her blood did flow.*
>
> *I took her by her golden curls,*
> *And I drug her 'round and 'round,*
> *Throwing her into the river,*
> *That flows through Knoxville town.*
> *Go down, go down, you Knoxville girl,*
> *With the dark and roving eyes,*
> *Go down, go down, you Knoxville girl,*
> *You can never be my bride.*

The reason why he kills her is right there. "Go down, go down, you Knoxville girl, with the dark and roving eyes," he says. That's the reason he kills her, her "dark and roving eyes." She's been looking around at too many other men.

And, of course, Willie doesn't get away with it. That's the way of it, as Ira and I learned at an early age from Papa, you don't get away with nothing. He goes home and loses his mind. He sees the flames of hell all around him, and spends the rest of his life in a dirty old jail.

It was the most requested song that we ever had. Anywhere we went, people would be yelling out for it before we even got our instruments tuned. Even after "I Don't Believe You've Met My Baby" was released and went to number one, we got five times more requests for "Knoxville Girl" than we did for our number one hit.

It almost seemed like a joke, we played it so many times. At any time, I could just say "Knoxville Girl," and everybody in the band would break out in a laugh. I know Ira got sick of singing it. I guess we all did.

I remember one time we'd driven God knows how many miles for this show in a bowling alley. When we walked in, I asked the manager, "Is there a dressing room?" And, of course, there was none. There was just a men's restroom. And while we were in there changing clothes, this drunk came in. You could tell he was way out of it. "By God," he said, all blustery, "y'all better play 'Knoxville Girl.' "

Well, Ira had found himself a bottle of whiskey somewhere and he was drinking some. And like all drunks, there was nothing Ira could stand less than another drunk. I've never understood that, but that seems like it's always the way it is. "Naw," Ira said, "that's one goddamn song we won't be playing tonight."

"I drove two hundred miles to see this show," the drunk said. "And I came to hear 'Knoxville Girl.' You better play it."

Of course, that pissed Ira off. "Let me tell you something, stupid," he said. "You might as well go out there, get your money back, and head on back to wherever you came from. You won't hear 'Knoxville Girl' tonight."

Well, the drunk's face turned all red, and I thought he was gonna throw a punch at Ira right there. But he didn't. He just said, "By God, I better hear it," and left the restroom.

Well, we got changed and got up onstage, but before we could get through with the first song, that drunk dude was standing up in the audience, hollering, "I want 'Knoxville Girl!' "

Ira stopped singing right in the middle of the song. "Security," he said. "I need security. Somebody give this asshole his money back and I'll repay you. I want this drunk out of here."

Before you know it, he was escorted out. I really don't know what happened to him because I didn't see him after the show was over. But I'll say that I always thought that was uncalled for on Ira's part.

Unfortunately, more than a few of our shows were under par like that. When he was straight, the show was top-notch. But when he was disabled on whiskey, the show was disabled, and it was just me and the picker doing the best we could. The shows were never as good then, they couldn't be.

That song, "Knoxville Girl," has made the complete rounds, though. All kinds of people have played it. There was even an actor, Billy Bob Thornton, who did a version not too long ago. I ran into him at Grimey's Record Store and he invited me to come to his show that night at Mercy Lounge, and since it didn't cost nothing, I went. Well, lo and behold, he got me onstage and we sang "Knoxville Girl" together. It was quite a bit different from the Louvin Brothers version, I'll say, but I like to think we established a little continuity between our different kinds of music.

One thing that Billy Bob Thornton told me was that in listening to the Louvin Brothers record, he never could tell who was leading the song, Ira or me. And the truth is that neither Ira nor I really ever did lead a song all the way through. We changed parts whenever we needed. Billy Bob thought that I was the one who sung the high tenor, and I said, "No, man, you sing it down here in this key and I can sing it with you, but I can't sing that high harmony."

For me, I still truly enjoy doing the tragic songs. The older

I get, the more they speak to me. Especially "Mary of the Wild Moor." I can't help but get teared up every time I hear that song.

But, of course, the tragedy of yesterday's songs is nothing compared to the tragedy we have today. You can talk about "Knoxville Girl" being a tragic song, but it only talks about the death of one person. Today the death of just one person wouldn't even make the news. Hell, if you had a wreck that killed ten people at the same time that would barely make the news today. Of course, it ain't bigger news one way or the other to the people that's lost somebody, but as far as the news items go, ten people barely matter, and one don't count at all.

But the greatest percentage of people who listen to real country music, they dig those sad old songs. They always have. There's tragedy in life, I guess is the reason. Sometimes I think there's more tragedy than there is life. And we need those old songs, even if nobody in new country music sings them anymore.

CHAPTER 34

DRUNKARD

I'd been watching Ira's drinking worsen since we started having hits. He'd always been something of a drinker, just like he'd always been something of a ladies' man. He'd started drinking when he was probably seventeen years old, but when we were starting out and didn't have no money, he kind of had to show some restraint. We had to work so hard that we never had time for bad habits, even if we could have afforded them. I don't think Ira drank anything during our early years except for beer.

As for me, I never really had the option of being an alcoholic. I always knew I had a whole bunch of people who believed in me, and I didn't want to disappoint them. Even when I do drink, and I've been known to drink a beer here and there, I buy my own. Every time. That way you can't go around telling people how you and Charlie Louvin got smashed together. I don't want to leave a legacy like that for my kids.

CHARLIE LOUVIN

We've had some others in Nashville that you never saw totally straight, that's for sure. George Jones was probably the worst. I worked a show with him once and we were standing back in the wings waiting to go on. He was acting a little peculiar, so I asked, "You been drinking, George?"

"Naw," he said. "I been working on my drinking problem."

"How's that?"

By way of an answer, he reached in his coat pocket, pulled out a handful of cocaine, and buried his nose in it, snorting. Then, when he'd fixed up that side of his nose, he went after the other.

George Jones and me

"How's that working for you?" I asked.

"Pretty good," he said. "Waylon told me it'd help."

George's wife, Nancy, is the only reason he's still alive. She hired a guard to follow him around everywhere he goes. He's as big as a bale of cotton. You wouldn't want to pick a fight with him without a Thompson submachine gun. If George is out somewhere and wants to go to the restroom, that guard goes with him. He stands right there and watches George take it out and piss, and then follows him back out. If you was in that restroom and was to say, "Would you like a drink, George?" you'd most likely lose an arm. That guard'd be on top of you like shit on stink.

That's the only way she could do it. She couldn't let him go anywhere, because everywhere he went some old George Jones buddy had a bottle. "Aw, come on," they'd say, "just one drink, George." And, buddy, if George ever took one, he was on one. Bless his heart, he didn't have a stopping place. If he took one sip, he'd stay with you until the bottle was gone, and if he drank one beer, you can bet that he'd get blind drunk before he quit.

Ernest Tubb had the same problem, but about two years before he died, he quit altogether. By that time, he and his wife were separated, and he was living in a motel room about two miles from where his house was, driving the ugliest little car you ever seen. If there was money anywhere, I don't know where it went. The only money he was spending went to the little restaurant he ate at and the price of the motel room. All his friends, me included, tried to talk him into coming to the Opry. But he wouldn't. He lived in that motel room for two years before he passed away and nobody ever seen him outside of it.

But even Ernest and George at their worst didn't drink like Ira. See, George was always just trying to have a good time, and Ira, he was never interested in a good time at all. It always looked like he was doing it to prove something. To let everybody know that nobody could tell him what to do. Or maybe to get even with somebody. I never knew exactly who. Papa, me, God. But somebody. It was an ugly thing when he drank, and there was no fun in it.

He got mean, too. When he drank whiskey, you wouldn't have known it was him except to look at him. The way he talked and acted, you'd see a true Jekyll and Hyde. You couldn't do nothing to please him. Those of us who got the tough end of it learned to just stand aside and not get hooked on any of his questions. And to pray that he didn't notice us.

His drinking started to affect our career. The worst was when he was drunk onstage. He felt like he was the master of ceremonies, "You just do what I tell you to do on the stage," he'd say, "and everything'll be cool." But then, the first thing you know, he'd look out at the audience and slur out, "Who the fuck let all these drunks in here?" And you knew right away it was gonna be a bad night. Some of the best MC work that was done on a Louvin Brothers show was done by me, just because I couldn't stand to hear him drunk and swearing, "Somebody kick out all these fucking drunks."

You'd think somebody who drank as he did would have some sympathy for folks out in the audience having a couple beers. But not Ira. The more he drank, the more he hated everybody else for drinking. Sometimes I thought it was because he knew they could do it and have fun, and I don't think he was capable. I'm not sure he ever had any fun in his life. He'd cuss out an entire audience at the drop of a hat.

He was getting us kicked off the Opry here and there. There was this place called Tootsie's Orchid Lounge in Nashville where everybody drank, and now and then it'd happen that Ira'd start fussing at somebody, and before you know it, it'd turn into a fracas. Then the papers would get ahold of it, and the Opry wouldn't want the Louvin name on the show for four or five weeks.

Probably the greatest single opportunity he cost us was when the television producer Al Gannaway came to Nashville to videotape everybody. Ira and I were scheduled to do fifty-two songs for him at a hundred dollars apiece, but the first day we went to the studio, Ira had his mandolin shined up like a pair of patent leather shoes, and this guy walked over to him with a spray can, looking to dull it down a little.

"What the hell do you think you're gonna do with that?" Ira said. He'd been out the night before, and I don't think he'd gotten any sleep at all.

"I'm gonna have to spray that mandolin," the guy said. "When it's shiny like that it'll black the camera out."

"You spray that shit on my mandolin," Ira said, "And I'll make a necktie out of it for you."

The guy went over and told Gannaway what Ira'd said. "What do you want me to do?" he asked him.

"We're just gonna have to take the chance that it won't black the camera out," Gannaway said. "But you can bet they won't be cutting but one session."

So we went out and did "Love Thy Neighbor as Thyself" and "I Don't Believe You've Met My Baby," and that was it. We lost fifty songs on that one deal alone. Plus the untold publicity it would have brought to the Louvin Brothers. I couldn't help but get tickled how Ira was so meticulous about his mandolin that he couldn't stand to see it get sprayed with something to dull down the shine, but if it got out of tune, he'd stomp it into splinters.

I tried to be a happy-go-lucky guy with him, and let the chips fall where they may, but it finally got to where that wouldn't work no more. And our fights got more frequent. One of the nastiest ones we ever had was that one back at our old Sand Mountain farm, when he called Mama a bitch.

When we got back to Nashville, Ira knew what he'd done wasn't right. That he shouldn't have called his own Mama a bitch. And then nothing wouldn't do but to drive all the way back down to Sand Mountain to set things right. He was ter-rified she'd be mad and wouldn't accept his apology, but he should have known better. I have no doubt but that's what she'd been dreaming. He stayed there two days, crying on her shoulder. Swearing he'd never drink again.

But an apology is worthless if it don't mean nothing to the person who's apologizing. If he's just gonna go screw up exactly the same way again. And Ira surely drank again, and was disrespectful with her more than once. Never bad enough to call her a bitch again, but he was disrespectful. And I was right on top of his head.

I truly believe that the one thing in life you oughta be respectful with is your mother. I believed it so strongly that every time he showed her any disrespect I whipped his ass.

CHAPTER 35

FRYING PAN

Ira did a lot of dumb things during this time in his life, but probably the dumbest thing he ever did was to get married a third time. I don't think any of us were sad to see his second wife, Bobbie, go when he divorced her, but after seeing him and Faye together, we might have traded her back. He had a thing for marrying women that weren't worth killing.

Faye was actually a good gal when Ira met her. A pretty girl, too. Just a slip of a thing, with dark hair and a shy little smile. He met her through her sister and brother-in-law, Smiley and Kitty Wilson, who played music with us. And when he first started courting her she was as sweet as could be. But before long, he'd taught her that you can't be sociable unless you take a drink. And he finally taught her so well that she could out drink him.

When they were sober, they were just as quiet as two church mice. But they weren't sober very often. It was just constant, the way they fought. One night she'd call me up and

Ira and me with Faye and Betty

say, "Ira's trying to kill me, I've got myself locked in the bathroom. Come help." So I'd have to go down to their house and
either calm everything down or fight him until he gave up.
And then, two nights later he'd call me from the bathroom
where he was locked in, and I could hear her smashing dishes
in the background, screaming about how she was gonna cut
his throat. And then, sure enough, I'd have to go again to talk
her down.

I told Ira at one point, "I'm gonna move so damn far
away you'll have to place a long distance call to get me." I
even tried a couple times, but it wasn't two months before

he moved right up within rock-throwing distance of us again.

One time, Betty drove Faye all the way up to Lincoln, Nebraska, to see Ira and me at a show. Bless her heart, Betty would always come visit me whenever she could, even if it just meant coming to meet me for a night. This time I wished she hadn't, though. On that short a visit, Ira and Faye got drunk and had a fistfight in their hotel room. Betty and I could hear them all night, fighting fists and teeth. It was just pathetic.

This other time Ira and Faye invited us up to their place for Sunday dinner. But when Betty and I pulled up in the driveway, he was beating the holy hell out of her right there in the yard. He had her on the ground and he was on top of her, laying into her head with whatever he could get ahold of. Rocks, clumps of dirt, sticks, anything.

It looked like he was gonna kill her, so I jumped out of the car, grabbed him by the hair of the head, and threw him over in the dust by the edge of the woods. Then, when I was holding him so he couldn't get back to her, I felt this explosion on my head. I didn't have any idea what it was, but it about knocked me out cold. When I opened my eyes, I saw Faye standing there with a cast-iron skillet in her hand, and it was cracked. She'd hit me so hard, she actually cracked the skillet.

Oh my Lord I was pissed. Somehow, I made it to my feet, and I pointed at her, holding my head with my other hand. "Woman," I said, "If you think I'll ever save your ass again, you're gonna wanna think twice."

"Aw, Charlie," she said, her eyes welling up with tears. "I'm so sorry."

"The hell you are," I said. "You cracked the damn skillet."

"I thought it was Ira," she said.

"No, you didn't think it was Ira," I said. "I was on top, and you ain't never seen Ira on top of me in a fight, ever. But next time, I'll sure as hell let him bump you off, that's for damn sure."

Even worse than having to break them up was that he used our house to get away from her. It got so that I even started keeping whiskey under the sink for when the bars closed. I never bothered buying beer, of course, because he didn't drink beer. But I'll bet I had ten different kinds of whiskeys down there.

Then, after a while, it wasn't just him stopping by. He'd bring his friends, too. And it got to where he wouldn't even say hello when he come through the kitchen door. He'd just go straight to the sink, open the door, get his favorite bottle out, and then starting passing bottles to all his friends. Only when they were absolutely sure that they'd had enough would they leave.

I finally told Betty one day, "We're really pissing away a lot of money under that sink, and we ain't making any friends. They're only coming here because the bars are closed."

A grin exploded across her whole face. That made her so happy she couldn't stand it, because she got to pour all the whiskey into the sink. And sure enough, when they all came by the following Saturday night after the bars closed, Ira never even said, "Hello," when he walked in. He just went straight for the sink. But when he pulled those doors open, it was as clean as a hounds' tooth. He turned around with a real weird look on his face, like, "What happened?"

Betty spoke up. "Charlie gave me permission to pour it all down the sink," she said brightly. "And then I ran a lot of water after it. But y'all come back to see us whenever you want." We never had another damn visitor on a late Saturday night. Which was fine by us.

I've always thought Ira was jealous of Betty and me, to tell the truth. Even though I would have hated to be a competitor to see who could get the most women, it drove him nuts that he couldn't hang onto one.

I'm proud that I stayed with the one I did. If I have anything at all to thank God for, it would be Betty. It took two and a half years to decide on her, but it was the wisest decision I ever made. We've had a good sober relationship, and we didn't spend any of our money on booze. She always would have rather been a half mile from it than any closer, and after she saw what it did to Ira, she learned to hate it.

I'm sure it was tough on her with all the traveling I did. I remember one year, Ira and I worked three hundred and thirty-five shows in one year, and put 170,000 miles on our car doing it. I don't know what we did with the thirty days we had off, but I have a strong feeling most of 'em was used for travel. Betty had to raise our kids practically by herself. And she did a hell of a job.

A lot of times I'd come home, and the first thing she'd do is tell me that she'd told one or another of them that I would whip his ass. But I never did have much stomach for that. I'd say, "Hey, I didn't come home to beat the kids. I come home to enjoy them." We had a few disagreements over that, but that's the way it is.

Ira just couldn't understand why Betty and I never fought the way he and Faye did. That really bothered him. "Everybody does it," he'd say.

"There's no future in it," I tried to tell him. "Nobody wins an argument. All you do is piss two people off when you start arguing. Then it gets loud and you say things you don't mean, and then you have to apologize later."

He didn't believe it, though. In his mind, if you didn't cuss and argue and fight, you didn't really love each other. But for me, I see it the other way around. There ain't nobody who's lived together as long as my wife and I have who's never had an argument, I ain't saying that, but you have to try to figure things out before the argument gets heated. You have to decide if it's worth the discussion, or if you're both just acting stupid.

We've been married for sixty-one years, Betty and I. That ain't a record, but it's pretty damn good for a hillbilly. I don't know why I've been allowed to keep the same woman for that long, but I thank God for it. And I do pity Ira that he never got to enjoy the kind of companion I had. But he made those choices.

CHAPTER 36

JIMMY CAPPS

Faye and I weren't the only ones Ira was hard on, either. He could be rough on the boys in our band. Especially our last guitar player, Jimmy Capps. We went through a few guitar pickers in our time. Our first was Chet Atkins, but then he became a big producer and an executive for RCA, and had about fifteen artists he was responsible for, so he didn't have time to record for people like us anymore. When he left, though, he found his replacement, Paul Yandell.

I don't know what it was about Paul, but we were mean to him. I mean, you get a band out on the road, and it doesn't take too long before everybody gets a little squirrelly. They start pulling jokes on each other, and then, the first thing you know, they're not jokes anymore. They're just hard down nasty. And we did some things that were hard down nasty to Paul.

Our worst pranks usually had to do with keeping him up for two or three days. We just wouldn't let him get no rest at all, and as soon as he did find a place to lay his head, one of us'd play a washtub outside his door or some silly thing. Probably the worst thing we ever did when we'd kept him up like that was to send the bellhop to his room with a sandwich that was made out of nothing but sardines pushed down into an inch of mayonnaise, two things we knew he couldn't stand. We told the bellhop to keep knocking until Paul answered the door, and to make sure he ate every bite of that sandwich. He didn't, though. Slung it right into the wall.

We didn't have Paul long enough to abuse him too much, though. The Army drafted him, and afterward we got Jimmy Capps, and he was with us the rest of our career. He was just a baby when he started with us. He couldn't have been more than nineteen years old, a slender, good-looking kid. I don't know if it was because he was so young or not, but he was ex- tremely fastidious about his clothes, which we used to make fun of him for all the time. Especially since we bought them for him. That was the way it was done at the time, the leader of a band usually bought their musicians clothing since they didn't make a whole lot of money.

Sometimes I wonder that he stuck with us so long, if you want the truth. There always seemed to be an explosion just about to happen. There was this one time, I remember, when we were playing this gig in Bartlesville, Oklahoma, with Jimmy C. Newman and Little Jimmy Dickens. It was at an armory, and it was one of those where each of us would go up and play an hour, and then they scooted the chairs back and it was dance time.

Well, we were singing a few love songs you could dance to, and Ira's mandolin went out of tune. And as always, he tried to tune it for about thirty seconds, but when he couldn't get it together, he just slung it back against the wall. Then, figuring that wasn't good enough, he went back and kicked it once, picked it up, and then stomped back into the dressing room. Of course, that left just Jimmy Capps and me standing

Ira, Jimmy Capps, and me

onstage by ourselves. But we went ahead and did our songs, finishing the hour.

When Capps and I got back in the dressing room, Ira was sitting there in a chair, with all the pieces of the mandolin piled on the floor. Just sitting there staring at them. Neither Capps nor I said anything to him. We knew better than that. We just went about our business, ignoring him.

But then Jimmy Dickens came in, grinning this wicked little grin he got. He spied the pile of mandolin pieces, walked over to it, picked up the neck, and propped it up on the steam grill. He was an agitating little prick, Dickens was. "Ira," he said, "I believe if you'll just stomp that neck right there, that ought to do it."

"Mind your own fucking business," Ira said. He stood and grabbed up what was left of it by the neck. "It's my mandolin. I'll do what I want with it."

"You proved that, didn't you?" Jimmy Dickens cackled.

"Fuck you," Ira said, and busted out of the room.

Well, after a show, the first thing Capps'd do is change into his street clothes and load his Val-A-Pak with his clothes in it in the car, so they wouldn't get mussed up. Unfortunately, on this night, Jimmy Capps had left his Val-A-Pak sitting on-stage, and when I came out of the dressing room after Ira, I caught him walking back and forth across it. Strutting and stomping, still holding that busted mandolin.

"Hey," I said, coming up on him. "Get off them fucking clothes. They belong to Jimmy Capps and he ain't done nothing to you."

"I know whose clothes they are," Ira said, and he kept stomping.

"Well, then get off 'em."

"By God," he said, "I bought 'em."

"It don't make no difference who bought 'em, they're his now," I said. "His to keep clean and looking nice. So stay off 'em."

"I'll do what the fuck I want with 'em," Ira said. "If he don't like it, he can buy his own."

"You don't make no sense," I said. "You didn't buy 'em to walk on. Besides I bought half of them, and I don't want my half walked on."

"Fuck you," he said. "Why don't you try to stop me?"

I'd had about enough of it at that point, so I reached out and grabbed him off the Val-A-Pak. He didn't like that at all, so he swung on me with the busted neck of his mandolin. I stuck up my arm to block, and the rest of the mandolin just peeled down my elbow. "That's it," I said. "Outside. I'm kicking your ass right now."

"You got it," he said. "Let's go."

As soon as I stepped out of the door, he swung at me. I dodged, got him by the hair of the head, and bounced his face off the ground. Then I jumped on top of him and starting hitting him. We were really getting with it when Jimmy C. Newman and Jimmy Dickens came out the door. Back in Newman's younger days, he was an extremely muscular man, and he just reached out and lifted me off Ira by the head. I mean, I was on top of Ira, putting his face through the ground, and he just reached down, got me by the crown of the head, and lifted me straight up. Ira started getting up, and Newman looked at him. "If either of you wants to whip somebody," he said, "you just try and whip me. I'd love to see either of you try it."

Neither of us wanted to fight Newman. We both knew that neither of us would have lasted a minute if we'd tried. But we all stood there cussing at each other. We were really raising a ruckus, but we didn't figure anybody could hear us out there in back of the armory. Then, all of the sudden, we were lit up by headlights.

We all kind of stopped talking and looked up, saw it was just some guy trying to get out of the parking lot, and went back to cussing. Well, the next thing we knew, the guy threw his car into park and stepped out. He was at least six foot six inches tall, bigger even than Jimmy Newman, and he walked right over to us and said, "Gentlemen, I got my wife out here in the car and I don't appreciate language like that."

Little Jimmy Dickens turned and stepped right up on him. I believe his nose came up to about that fella's navel, but he didn't care. He stood right up on him and put his finger and thumb almost together, and said, "Mister, you're just about this far from having me all over your ass."

Well, that old boy just looked down at Dickens for a minute, then he pushed him out of the way and walked back to his car, and he and his wife spun their wheels getting out of there. That was it. We all started laughing and we couldn't stop.

That's stuck with Dickens for all these years, too. You can go up to him at any time and put your finger and your thumb together, and he knows exactly what you're talking about. Still today, if he says something that somebody doesn't want him to talk about, they'll say, "Jimmy, you're just about that far from having me all over your ass."

Dickens was mean, though. If he fought you, he could slip up between your legs and de-ball you before you knew what happened. He was a dangerous fighting man because he was so low down. He whipped Webb Pierce once, I'll never forget that. Webb weighed over two hundred pounds, and Dickens beat him up bad.

Little Jimmy Dickens at a towering 4 foot 11 inches

CHAPTER 37

DUETS

Somehow, Ira and I managed to remain some kind of friends even with all that fighting. I don't know how we did it, though. Most of the other brother duets didn't get along at all. I remember when the Everly Brothers were installed in the Country Music Hall of Fame, only Phil showed up. I even asked him, "Where's Don at?"

"He has some family sick," he said. "He's back in Texas taking care of them."

That was bullshit, of course, but they weren't alone in hating each other. There were duets that put out the most beautiful music you could imagine, but when they weren't on-stage, they wouldn't speak to each other. And they wouldn't speak to you, either, if you happened to like the other one. If you wanted to be friends with one, you had to hate the other.

I think that's silly, of course. I might have somebody I hate with all my heart, but they could live and die and never know it. You're just spinning your wheels when you hate somebody. You're better just to try to get over it. You don't have to become bed brothers with your enemy, but you don't hurt nobody but yourself when you hate. That's why I try not to have a hate list.

I went to see Earl Bolick once. He was one of the Blue Sky Boys, a duet that inspired Ira and me back when we were kids. I'd never met either one of them and I wanted to, so when I was passing through Atlanta one time, I knocked on his door, introduced myself, and he welcomed me into his home. Then, after we'd sat and talked for a while, I made the mistake of asking, "How's your brother, Bill?"

He got this kind of funny look on his face, and said, "Well, I see we've run out of things to talk about."

I knew it was time to move on then. I don't know why, but they really disliked each other. Neither one of them would have saved the other one from a fire if they could have pulled them out.

The worst was the Monroe Brothers, though. Lord, they hated each other. Most of it was because of their women, too. Their wives would get to fighting among themselves and get the men involved. Bill's wife would call up Charlie and say, "I heard what your wife said about me. Bill's gonna come over to your house and break every bone in your body with a ball bat."

"Tell him to come on," Charlie would say. "I've got a ball bat, too."

So Bill would. He'd go over to Charlie's house, Charlie would come out of the house, and they'd fight in the front yard with fucking ball bats. And then they'd go out on the road and sing together.

There's more, too. Teddy and Doyle of the Wilburn Brothers didn't get along. And the Delmore Brothers didn't get along, either. It seemed like in every duet, there'd be one of them that was a drinker. In the Delmore Brothers, it was

Rabon, and in the Wilburn Brothers, it was Doyle. You'd think two brothers from the same family would be something alike. But it never worked out that way.

The only duet I can think of that made it was the Osborne Brothers. At least until a medical procedure took Sonny out. He got a new shoulder put in, and after the surgery, his fingers would go down the neck of his banjo as he was picking, but they couldn't make his hand go back up. So he just quit. Told his brother, Bobby, "Banjo playing is half of my act, and I can't do it. Get you somebody that can." So Bobby got a kid from Detroit, but he don't call it the Osborne Brothers anymore. He calls it Bobby Osborne & the Rocky Top Press. He's still in the business, though.

Maybe what saved Ira and I from becoming true enemies was the fights were so one-sided. Ira just couldn't fight at all. There were times I almost felt bad for him for his lack of

Taking different trains

fighting ability. It was the same as picking cotton. He was six foot tall and kind of gawky, and before he could really try to make a move, I already had him whipped. It might not be much of a feather in my cap, but I could whip his ass anytime, and he knew it.

I remember one night, we'd played in Oklahoma, and Porter Wagoner and Pretty Miss Norma Jean were on the show. Well, Ira thought that Norma Jean wanted to screw him, so even though we were all done and Porter Wagoner hadn't even gone on yet, he was trying to hang around to wait on her.

That's the way he was. He probably screwed more women than you could haul in a freight train, and if he thought a girl wanted to screw him, he'd miss any show date to fulfill that obligation. He always felt he was a ladies' man. You can tell it in the pictures of us, if you look. He never took a relaxed photograph, it was always posed. If you study the photographs that were made of Ira and I, you can see that he was more interested in the camera than anything else in the room.

The problem that time was that we didn't have time to mess around with Pretty Miss Norma Jean or anyone else. "Ira," I told him, "We're in North Carolina tomorrow. We can't afford to kill any time here. We got to go now."

Well, he'd been drinking, and that pissed him off to no end. But we had to go. A lot of people don't understand what wasting one hour in one place can do to you ten hours out yonder. In ten hours, you may be praying for that one hour back, but once it's gone, it's gone. I've always believed that if you have a long haul, you do the best you can in the beginning, and don't let up. If you get there early, that's when you can rest.

So we left, and drove out of town about ten miles before we came up on this little burger joint. I hadn't eaten anything, and I was getting awful hungry, so I pulled into the lot. "I thought you didn't have time to waste," Ira said, sulking.

"At least not for me. But now you got time to get something to eat, don't you?"

"People have to eat, Ira," I said. "Come on in and get you something. It might help you."

"I don't want any fucking thing to eat," he said.

"I think maybe you could use something in your stomach," I said. But I knew better than to try to reason with him, so I shut the door, and ran in to get some food. And, since it was cold out, the middle of winter, I left the motor running to keep him from freezing to death.

Then, as I was standing at the counter waiting for the food, I heard this noise. We were driving this little old Corvair, something like a station wagon, but with an air-cooled engine, and I realized what I was hearing was the engine revving up. I walked over to the door and looked out, and there Ira was, jamming his foot down on the accelerator, holding the engine as wide open as it went.

Next to me at the counter was a cop. I turned to him and said, "Mr. Officer, would you do me a favor?"

The cop nodded. "Yessir, what is it?"

"That drunk out there behind the steering wheel is my brother, and I believe he's trying to blow my engine up. Could you go out there and have a word with him?"

"Sure thing, mister," the cop said, and he walked out, straight to the car, and opened the back door. I don't know exactly what he said to Ira, but I do know he told him that he could either get in the backseat of his own car and act right, or he could ride in the backseat of the cop's car all the way to jail. Ira chose his own backseat, and he was sitting back there wide awake and bolt upright when I came out with the hamburgers. Lord, was he pissed.

I didn't talk, Jimmy Capps didn't talk, and Ira didn't talk. Not for hours. We had an all-night haul to make it to North Carolina, and they finally fell asleep, so I just kept driving.

Then, sometime around four o'clock in the morning, Ira suddenly jerked awake. "I got it," he said. "I finally figured out a way to whip your ass."

I couldn't help it, I started to laugh. And then Jimmy Capps started laughing, too. And finally, even Ira got tickled and started to laugh as well.

We never did hear what his big idea was, though. Waking up, he'd forgotten it.

As far as I know, that was the end of the Ira Louvin and Norma Jean affair, too. At least, I never heard of them going at it. I'll bet Ira died pissed off because he didn't get it from her.

That was the way he was, though. Whenever he saw a woman that really turned him on, he'd kill himself trying to figure out a way to get with her. I don't care if it was a grandma, he'd do his damnedest to figure out a way to make it happen.

It'd get him trouble now and then, too. Once we were working a dance in Buzzard Roost, Texas, and some guy came over and asked Ira, "Buddy, would you do me a great favor?" He was a big old boy, as tall as Ira, but about twice as broad.

"If I can, I will," Ira said.

"My wife really wants to dance with you," the guy said.

"She does?" Ira said. "Which one is she?"

"That's her right there," the guy said, pointing. And she was a real beauty. Had to be the prettiest woman in Buzzard Roost, anyway.

"I don't know if it's a good idea," Ira said, but he was still looking at her, ogling her, really, and I could already tell how this was gonna end.

"Aw, there's nothing to it," the guy said. "Just do me a favor and dance with her for one song."

Well, Ira got out there and started to dance with her. And as the song wore on, they kept moving a little closer together. Right up until that guy walked out on the dance floor, grabbed Ira's shoulder, and just knocked the shit out of him. Laid him out on the floor.

"What the hell's wrong with you, man?" I said. "You talked him into it."

"I asked him to dance with her," the guy said. "Not fuck her on the dance floor."

CHAPTER 38

MANDOLINS

Even with all the fussing and fighting, Ira's drinking didn't get real bad until this one incident with Ken Nelson. See, there was almost nobody Ira trusted with his music. Even Fred Rose, who'd helped Hank Williams write some of his best songs, wasn't allowed to give him any criticism. Rose could say something about how maybe we could just change one word, and Ira would crumple up the song and throw it in the trash can. "If you don't like it, I'll write you another," he'd say. And he would.

The only person he could really work with was Ken Nelson. He even looked to Ken for advice from time to time. Sometimes, it seemed, even approval. One time, I remember, we were in the studio recording a gospel song called "Born Again." We'd sung this song dozens of times together and at this one part I would drop way down and Ira would go way up and then we'd swoop in the other direction and meet in the middle. That part had come of remembering the girl at that Sacred Harp reunion so long ago, with the voice that would soar into the treetops, and then swoop down on you when you least expected it.

After the session, Ken Nelson jumped Ira. "Good God, what was that thing you did in there?" he asked. He looked almost flustered.

"What thing?" Ira asked.

"That thing where you went way up and Charlie went way down and then you came back together."

Ira shrugged, but you could tell he was pleased Ken had noticed it. "I don't know," he said. "It was just something I heard once upon a time, and I thought it would sound good. You want me to take it out?"

"Oh, hell no," Ken said. "I love the sound. I just wanted to know what you called it."

"I honestly don't know," Ira said. He was beaming just like a little kid getting praise from his Papa, busting all over with pride.

Along with that, for all he mistreated his mandolins, Ira was proud of his playing. Really proud of it. He'd taught himself, and he'd become one of the best mandolin players in Nashville by his own hard work. Sometimes I think that's why he broke them onstage like he did. Sure, he was usually drinking, but I always thought it was because he felt betrayed by them when they'd go out of tune. It was as if he thought they were doing it to him on purpose.

That's why every time Ira smashed one of his mandolins, you'd see him with a paper sack and a little broom after the show, sweeping every little splinter of it up. And six months down the road, you'd see that same mandolin, and there wouldn't be a scratch on it. He'd have glued it all back together, splinter by splinter, and spray painted it again right back to its original color. You couldn't find a blemish on it.

But unfortunately, country music was starting to suffer

because of rock and roll, and some people thought it had something to do with the old timey instruments like the mandolin. It wasn't, it was Elvis, but people were trying to find anything they could that they could fix, and you couldn't really fix Elvis.

Anyway, everybody's record sales were hurting. And there was nobody it enraged more than Ira. He came home one night and found Terry and Kathy, the two children he had with Faye, watching American Bandstand on television, and he kicked a hole in the screen. For my part, I didn't worry about it too much. There wasn't much I could do about it, I figured, and we were making a living.

But everybody was scrambling for a way to bring country record sales up again. There was a kind of panic all over Nashville. And one time we were in the studio, and Ken Nelson, Ira's most trusted friend, said to him, "Ira, I do believe it's your mandolin that's slowing down the sales of Louvin Brothers records."

The whole studio just went silent. Nobody spoke. And then Ira just put his mandolin back in its case. No fussing or cussing like you'd expect, he just put it back in its case.

But after that, he never did another mandolin intro, another turnaround, nothing. The next time we recorded a song, I tried to encourage him. "This song'd be great with a mandolin intro, Ira," I said.

"No," Ira said. "Let the piano or one of the guitars do it. I'd hate to hurt the sales of Louvin Brothers records."

"Don't feel that way," I said.

"I don't need to feel that way," he said. "I've been told that way. There won't be no more mandolin features on a Louvin Brothers record. Not by me." And he stuck with it right until the end.

Afterward, Ken Nelson denied the whole thing. "I did not say that," he'd say. "I never said anything like that." But

I know he said it. I was right there, and there were at least eight more people in the studio, too. And he should have known better than to say it. Ira's talent came with some heavy costs, and one of those costs was that insecurity about himself. He'd taught himself how to do all of it. How to write songs, how to play the mandolin, how to sing in that high tenor. He'd done it all himself. And he just couldn't stand to see someone else judge it. In a way, it was all he had. Since he was a kid, playing those instruments and singing those songs were all he could count on to make his life worth something.

That one comment sped up Ira's drinking more than anything. He went from drinking too much on a Saturday night to putting down a fifth of whiskey a day, with beer on top of it. He was never sober after that. The way he treated his mandolins got worse, too. He still played them onstage, but you'd think he hated them the way he smashed them. It was more complicated than that, though. I don't think he could really be at ease playing the mandolin after what Ken Nelson said, and I don't think he could be at ease without playing it, either.

When the drinking got real bad, Betty and I tried to take him to a psychiatrist to see if that might help him. But the shrink turned out to be a Louvin Brothers fan, so instead of working with him on the drinking, he just asked him a whole bunch of questions about the different songs he'd written. And when he did finally get around to asking him, "Do you drink?" Ira just lied.

"Yeah," he said. "A little."

"How much would you say you drink a day? Half a pint?"

"Yeah, something like that," he said. And I knew that trip was pointless.

I didn't feel like I could just give up on him, though, so I got him to check into rehab. There was this place out east by the Nashville airport that somebody had told me didn't have no bars on it, but could help a man quit if he wanted to. So Betty and I somehow talked Ira into going, and he did real good there for a little while. But then Faye slipped him in a pint of whiskey for Christmas, and he drank it and walked out the next day.

I should've taken a shovelhead and beat the shit out of her. But some people will use a drinker's habit to their own advantage. And that woman did. Every time they'd get drunk and get in a fight, he'd buy her something. She couldn't afford for him to get sober.

That was about all I could do. The thing is, I don't know how to handle a drunk. I didn't know then, and I don't know now. I can insult one, I'm pretty good at that. But insulting a drunk just brings on something else, and usually they want to fight. And, hell, they can't fight good if they're drunk, so it's embarrassing.

Out on the town

CHAPTER 39

SATAN
IS
REAL

Even though we were singing more and more secular songs, and making good money at it, we never did stop doing the gospel stuff. We wrote a lot of songs that got used for altar calls, and I still get fan mail from people who swear up and down that the Louvin Brothers music saved their life. I doubt if God'll give us any credit for that though. I fear that we have to do more than write words for the big reward, but it was nice to know that our songs helped a person or two.

Most of our gospel songs weren't really guilt songs, but they were obvious songs. They'd tell you that if you're a good person, a righteous person, then you can go to heaven. But if you think you can do anything you want and still go to heaven, you're full of shit. God's always right there when you think you're getting away with something. There's nothing that escapes him and nothing he doesn't know.

Even a song like "The Great Atomic Power" is about those choices people make. The idea for the song was Buddy

Bain's, but he wasn't having no luck getting it down the way he wanted, so Ira took it off him. The way Ira wrote it was to remind everybody running around scared about nuclear bombs that if they was living how they oughta live, then there wasn't nothing to be scared of. That was what the song said, that there's only one way to escape the mushroom cloud, and that's to be ready to meet the Lord.

Another good example is the song "Satan Is Real." It doesn't insinuate nothing to the listener, it speaks very plainly. If there's a heaven, and everybody'd like to believe there's a heaven, then there has to a hell. Just like if there's a God, then there has to be a Satan. Half of it can't be true. That's what the song's about.

It has one of Ira's best recitations in it, where a guy stands up in a congregation to tell the preacher, "Hey, I know you like to talk about God, but Satan is real, too, so you might wanna figure that into your equation." It's a great speech, and once we got done with it we just knew it was gonna be the title song for our next album. In fact, I don't think there'd be a preacher in the United States that could have done it more effectively than Ira. You couldn't tell Ira's narrations from a sermon. You could hear his old preacher's calling coming out in him. It was sad, too, because he wasn't living nothing like what he was singing about.

We wrote six of the songs on that album, Ira and I. I was the idea man when it came to writing. He was the more gifted writer and I was the lesser when it came to talent from up above, but any writer needs a subject, so I kept my ear to the ground, and if I heard anybody say anything that sounded like a song title, I'd write it down and give it to Ira. If you gave him a good subject, he could write up lyrics in about fifteen minutes, and after that, we'd work out the tune together. We just made sure that harmonies would fit.

Ira took it upon himself to design the cover for *Satan Is*

Real, and he had it in his head that he wanted to put a real Satan on the cover. Well, my oldest boy Sonny had this Lionel Train we'd bought him, and it was attached to a four-by-eight sheet of plywood. And since neither Ira nor I had any money at the time to go buy a brand new sheet of plywood, we removed Sonny's train, and sawed the four-by-eight down the middle, cutting the devil out of that. It was sixteen feet tall when we finished, and we painted it ourselves, and then made the pitchfork and horns from the scraps.

After we got Satan built, Ira knew just where to put him. There was this abandoned rock quarry by my house that he thought would be perfect. So we set him up, and then went around and collected a bunch of old tires, and stacked them all around him. When the photographer for Capitol Records showed up, we had it all ready to go. We met him at our house and led him up to the place where we wanted the picture taken. And when he said he was ready, we poured kerosene into the tires and lit them on fire.

Wouldn't you know it, right about the time the photographer got ready to take the picture, it started sprinkling rain. Big drops. "We're gonna have to put this off," he said, starting to pack his camera away.

"The hell we are," Ira said. "We got the fires going, it's now or never."

"I don't want to get my camera wet," he said.

"I don't give a shit about your camera," said Ira. "If we can stand out here in these white monkey suits, it ain't gonna hurt your precious camera."

"All right, all right." The photographer grumbled.

All of a sudden, there was this big cracking sound, and we all jumped about a foot in the air. Then there was another, like an explosion. And another. It sounded like we were being shelled. We were all jerking around trying to figure out what was going on. And then Ira got it. "It's the rocks," he said.

Sure enough, it was. When a big drop of rain'd hit the rocks where the fire was burning, they were blowing like they had a stick of dynamite inside of 'em they were so hot. They were blowing pieces of rock as big as your fist fifty feet up in the air.

"You can't expect me to take pictures in this," the photographer said.

"That's exactly what I expect," Ira said. And he couldn't stop grinning.

Well, the photographer took the picture. And he even won some kind of award for it, but shit, he didn't have nothing to do with it but to aim the camera. You won't find anywhere on the album where it says the design of this album was by the Louvin Brothers. People collect it now, though. Back when the album was first released, I could have bought artist's copies for seventy-five cents. Today, if you can find that album for sale, it'll be five hundred dollars. That's about as cheap as you can buy an original Capitol Records' *Satan Is Real*.

I think my favorite song on the album is "Are You Afraid to Die?" In fact, it's one of my favorite Louvin Brothers songs ever. Most people will tell you they're afraid to die. At

least they should be. If you're a Christian, you never do really know where you stand, if you're being honest.

I don't know if Ira was afraid to die or not. One time I walked in on a conversation he was having with Betty that made me wonder. I tried not to let him spend a whole lot of time around her if I could help it, but when we were planning that *Satan Is Real* cover he was always over at the house. They were standing in the kitchen when I walked in, and he was saying, "Prove to me there's a God. If you're so sure of it, give me some proof."

Well, you could see by her face that she knew how impossible that was, so she said the only sensible thing to say, "Look around you, Ira. Look at the mountains, the trees, the rivers. If that don't tell you that there's a supreme being, I don't have the answer to what you're asking."

He seemed to take that for an answer. At least it ended the conversation. He spotted me standing there watching them, and we got back to work. It must have been on his mind, though, because only a day or two later, he said to me out of nowhere, "You know what we oughta do?"

"No idea," I said. "Whyn't you tell me?"

"We oughta quit fucking around with these drunks and just play churches," he said. "We oughta quit doing the secular shit and only play gospel." You could tell that it was worrying him. That he understood the difference between what he sang and how he lived.

I encouraged him when he said that, but I knew better than to get hopeful about it. He was very much against what he called begging, and when we played churches, that's what it would always turn into. The preacher would have to pry the money out of the congregations, saying things like, "These boys have number one records, they could be at any beer joint in town making pocketfuls of money, but here they are down at this church singing their guts out, and you people are throwing nickels and dimes. What's wrong with the world?" It did turn into begging. It was embarrassing.

The thing about Ira was that he had a gift for songwriting, true, but he also had another gift that interfered with his songwriting. It was that calling to be a preacher. He knew the Bible, and the way he wrote his songs, the material that was in the songs, the way he placed it and used it, he would have been tremendous. Everybody on Sand Mountain always told me that was the cause of his drinking problem. That he was called to be a preacher, but refused, becoming a picker and grinner instead, and trying to drown out the call with liquor and women.

I don't think that's the whole story, but I think it's part of it. The worldly things were just too strong for him. He couldn't overcome them long enough to be what he knew he ought to be, and that made his entire life a buildup of the misery in his mind. It haunted him that he didn't do what he was put here on this earth to do.

He tried to reflect his call to preach in his recitations, and I've had numerous people tell me that his recitations helped them turn their lives around, but that's nothing more than what we're all supposed to do. All of us should leave behind a few people that we really went out of our way to help. Ira was good on advice, but most of it was only in song.

Once in a while, you could get him to really talk in the way he believed, and it was a hundred and eighty degree angle from the kind of life he lived. But it's easy to talk, and it's hard to do God's work.

The good book says in several places that either you can serve the devil or you can serve God. You can't serve both at the same time. Many people try, sure. When they're at a hillbilly joint on Saturday night, they'll drink their beer and sing their go-to-hell songs, and then when they get in church on Sunday they'll try to convince the congregation that they're devout Christians. And a lot of people will be deceived by that. But at the end of time, you'll have those people you deceived on one hand, and the One who you didn't on the other. And that One will be the only hand that matters.

I don't think it's right to say that it was only ignoring that call to be a preacher that set Ira on the wrong path, though. I've always thought that maybe it had something to do with those beatings he got from Papa, too. Just like I've always thought that part of what made Papa so mean with us was the treatment he got from his Papa.

Maybe Ira thought that Papa beat him so much because he knew he was just plain bad. And maybe knowing that, Ira just plain gave up trying to do the right thing. Or maybe it was just that Ira understood how unfair it was that he was the main target of Papa's beatings, so he spent the rest of his life trying to spit in Papa's eye. He knew what Papa thought of alcohol and philandering, and it wouldn't take too much stretching of your mind to believe that he liked rubbing Papa's face in it.

People always said that it was like Ira was trying to get even with somebody when he drank, and maybe Papa was the one he was trying to get even with. And maybe he was trying to get even with Mama and me a little, too, for never stopping those beatings. And maybe we deserved it.

CHAPTER 40

SHE FINALLY DONE IT

It was a pretty normal night. Betty and I had got the dishes cleaned up and the children off to bed, and I was just sitting down on the couch fixing to light my last cigarette of the night. It was early, only about nine thirty, but when I was home, I liked to turn in at a reasonable hour when I could. And this was one of the few times when we had a place far enough from Ira's that we didn't have to worry about him stopping by. We were in Fairview, which was about forty miles from his home in Madison. Even if he and Faye was to start fighting, I couldn't have made it to their place in time to do anything about it.

Then the telephone rang. "Hello," I answered.

"Is this Charlie?" The man sounded familiar, but I couldn't place him. Whoever it was, his voice sounded thick, like maybe he'd been drinking.

"This is Charlie. Who's this?"

"It's Shot Jackson." That cleared it up. Shot Jackson was one of the best dobro and steel guitar players in Nashville.

"How you doing, Shot?" I asked.

"It's a goddamn mess, Charlie," he said. "She finally done it."

"Who finally done what, Shot?"

"Faye. Faye done it."

He'd definitely been drinking. "Done what, Shot?"

"She shot Ira, Charlie. Six times."

"Well, do me a favor," I said. "Call me if he dies." And then I hung up.

"Who was that on the phone?" Betty asked me, sitting down on the couch with me.

"Shot Jackson," I said.

"What did he want?" Betty asked.

"Just trying to play one of his practical jokes," I said. "Sounded like he'd been drinking, and even sober I wouldn't trust him standing on a stack of bibles."

Then, just as I said it, the phone rang again. "Hello?" I answered.

"Is this Mr. Louvin?" It was a woman's voice.

"This is Charlie Louvin, yes."

"I'm calling from the Nashville Memorial Hospital in Madison. We have your brother here in need of medical attention, and we need someone to sign for the bill."

I felt the blood drain out of me. "What happened?" I asked.

"He's been shot."

"I'll be there as soon as I can," I said.

Well, at that time, I owned a new Mercury station wagon, and I raced down the highway at seventy-five miles an hour, praying for a cop to pick me up and escort me to the hospital. I drove like a genuine, twenty-four-carat idiot, but when I got there, Smiley Wilson, Faye's brother, had already signed him in, and he and Roy Acuff and Shot were waiting on news in the lobby.

I finally got the story out of them. Or as much as I could. It was a jumbled up thing. As near as I could figure, Roy, Shot, and Smiley were over at Ira and Faye's house getting drunk, and for some reason Ira and Faye started fussing at each other. Trying to be respectful of their guests, I guess, they took their argument into the bedroom, and before you knew it, he had a telephone cord around her neck and was trying to choke her to death.

Well, Faye remembered that Ira kept a little .22 pistol under the pillow, and somehow managed to get her hands on it. She shot him in the left arm first, then again in the chest, and when he turned around to run, she shot him three more times in the back. And then walked up on him and shot him once more in the front, for good measure.

Lucky for him, none of the bullets went deep enough to hit his vital organs. They managed to get most of them out at the hospital, but the three she'd shot into his back were too close to his spine to be removed without paralyzing him, so they sealed them in there and hoped for the best. He carried them with him until he died.

Probably the worst thing was the statement she made to the cops. "If the sonofabitch don't die, I'll shoot him again." The newspapers got a hold of that, and so did the radio announcer, Paul Harvey. The next day I was listening to Harvey's show, and I heard him say, "Ira Louvin and his wife were up drinking last night, and she shot him six times with a .22 pistol. Then she told the police, 'If the blankety-blank don't die, I'll shoot him again.'" And then Harvey gave one of his little pauses like he did, and continued, "And he ain't dead yet."

Ira stayed in the hospital for a week. But in the middle of that week was the plane crash that killed Cowboy Copas, Hawkshaw Hawkins, and Patsy Cline. Ira knew all of them, and wouldn't nothing do but that he had to go down to the funeral home and see their bodies. So I found the doctor and asked him, "Is there any way we could pull that off?"

"It's probably not a good idea," he said.

"I know that," I said. "But he's got it in his head, and ain't nothing else gonna satisfy him."

The doctor sighed. "All right," he said. "Have him put on a stretcher board and tie him down so that he can't move his head. He can stay ten minutes, but then you bring him straight back."

So I fixed everything up, and then went back into Ira's room. "I've got an ambulance that'll take you, no charge," I said. "And I have a doctor that'll go with you. But we can't stay but ten minutes once we get there, and I'll be the one that's watching the clock."

"I'm not sure I like that," he grumbled.

"That's funny, I'm not sure you have a choice," I said. "In fact, I'm pretty sure you don't."

"All right," he grumbled.

So they loaded him on a stretcher, tied him down, put him on one of those roller carts, and wheeled him out to the ambulance. The only problem was that he couldn't turn his head to see into the caskets from the stretcher. So the people at the funeral home were nice enough to take one of their big round mirrors off the wall and stand on the other side of the casket so he could see what was in there. And we stayed ten minutes. No more.

The worst was yet to come, though. When Ira got out of the hospital, I'd hoped that would be the end of his and Faye's fussing at each other. I figured they'd get divorced, which seemed like a pretty good idea. But their fighting didn't even slow down, and it wasn't too long after Ira finally got well that he called me up on the telephone. "Charlie," he said. "I need you to do me a big favor."

I'll admit that by then I was a little leery of doing Ira any big favors, but I said, "All right, Ira, if I can."

"I want you to put that bitch in the crazy house," he said.

"Faye?"

"Hell, yes, Faye. She's crazy as a loon. I can't live with her no more."

I breathed in and held it for a few seconds, then let it out. "Are you absolutely sure that's what you want, Ira?"

"She shot me six times," he said. "If that don't mean she's crazy, what would?"

"You'd both been drinking," I said. "You fight when you drink."

"I ain't never shot anybody when I've been drinking," he said. "Not even once, let alone six times."

"I don't know," I said.

"Well, I do," he said. "They won't let me put her in there. But you can do it as family. If anybody gives you any trouble about it, you can tell 'em I was the one that wanted it."

I wanted nothing to do with it. The way they fought, it was only a matter of time before one of them tried to kill the other. Besides which, he'd been trying to choke her to death, and shooting him didn't seem entirely unsensible to me. Hell, I've always kept a gun around pretty much everywhere I go. I'm not wild, a guy'd have to shit on me pretty good to get shot, but if some big guy wants to come change the looks of my face, I will put a bullet in his ass. Fuck with my family and you can be dead, too. Some things I don't waver on, and I had a hard time thinking too poorly of Faye for what she done.

But Ira always had a way of getting me to do what he wanted, all the way back to fetching him the hatchet to chop down that damn persimmon tree so many years ago. And he wheedled and whined and begged, until somehow I found myself talking to a doctor who said he'd help me out. They came out, picked her ass up, and took her to the Middle Tennessee Mental Health Institute, right there in south Nashville.

Well, two or three days after I had her committed, Kitty and Smiley Wilson went to see her in the hospital, and then they went to talk to Roy Acuff. And once Roy heard where she was, he went straight to Ira and gave him all kinds of hell. "Goddamn, you shouldn't have done that, Ira," Roy said. "You know the only reason that bullshit happened was because of all the drinking. That woman ain't crazy, and there ain't no way in hell you should have had her put in there. Especially when you was trying to kill her first."

"I didn't have nothing to do with it," Ira said, playing dumb. "Charlie put her in there, not me. He's always had it out for her."

Well, Roy believed it. Just like that. And he started going around telling everybody in Nashville how I'd had Faye put in the mental hospital for no reason. And it being Nashville, everybody believed it of me, of course. It finally got to where I couldn't let it go on anymore, so I went and told Acuff the whole sorry story, how Ira had talked me into having her committed.

"I should have known it." Roy shook his head. "Well, what are we gonna do, Charlie? She ain't crazy."

"I've called down there to talk to them," I said. "Turns out it's a lot harder to get somebody out of a mental institution than it is to have 'em put in."

"We can't leave her in there," he said.

"The only thing I could think of is to ask the governor," I said. "I don't know him, he owes me nothing. But you know him pretty well, and I gotta think he could get it reversed."

Roy thought for a while. "I can't leave her in there," he said, finally. "I'll talk to him."

He did talk to the governor, and he got her out, thankfully. She wasn't real happy with me for a while, though. I don't think she talked to me up until her and Ira finally got divorced in 1964. There's no doubt that I was the asshole in that deal. I should have never gone along with Ira's request. Never. Like so many times before, I knew better, I just did it anyway.

Faye and I did finally become half-ass friends before she died, though. And I've always been happy we did. Cancer of the brain killed her, poor woman. She was bald-headed and blind when she passed.

Checking my revolver

CHAPTER 41

A LOAN

We lost a lot of money because of that shooting. We couldn't play shows, and things got real lean. While Ira was recuperating, it left me responsible for all the Louvin Brothers bills. So I did what I could, but we were still pretty far in debt by the time he was ready to work again.

Then, when he was finally well enough to hit the road, we had what I hoped would be a tremendous stroke of good luck. Our booker somehow managed to get us on a tour to Florida with Johnny Cash, Merle Travis, and the Carter Family. It probably wasn't nearly enough to get us out of debt, not even if every single show sold out. But it was a start, and I was happy to be working again.

Unfortunately, the first date didn't have nearly the kind of attendance that any of us were hoping for. Which left me sitting in my dressing room afterward, smoking a cigarette and trying not to think about it, when Johnny Cash poked his head in the door. "Hello, Charlie," he said. "I just got done playing and thought I'd stop by to see if you needed anything."

"I don't think so, John," I said, shaking my head. "We're just happy to be working. But thank you."

"All right," he said, and he got that look he got, like he just couldn't get comfortable in his own skin. "Well, maybe we'll do a little better tomorrow night."

"I sure hope so, John," I said.

He let it drop there, and closed the door to the dressing room.

Well, the next night we didn't do so well, either. I don't know what was going on, but nobody was showing up at all. And here comes John again. "Hello, Charlie," he said, opening the door.

"Hello again, John."

"I was just stopping by to see if you needed anything."

Well, he had a cigarette in his hand, and I was out. "I'll tell you what," I said. "You got an extra cigarette?"

"Yeah, sure." He pulled out his pack of cigarettes and dunked me out one. The brand was Home Run, as I recall, which I'd never had before.

It'd been a couple hours since I'd had a cigarette, so when I lit that thing and sucked in, I must've pulled an ash a hundred feet long. And it was, bar none, the strongest cigarette I'd ever had. I couldn't cough, I couldn't blow it out, I couldn't do nothing. I just froze up, choking, thinking I was gonna die.

John just laughed his ass off. "You want another one right quick before the taste goes away?" he asked, offering me the pack.

"No, thank you." I was pounding my chest, trying to get my breath back. "I believe I'll run out to the store and get my own."

"Well," he said, and he sort of shifted around in his jacket like all of the sudden it didn't fit right. "Do you need anything else?"

"No, John," I said. "I believe I'm all right. Just waiting on the crowds to start pouring in."

"They will," John said. "They will."

"Thank you, John. I sure hope so."

He let it drop again, and closed the door.

The next night when he stopped by, he finally came out with it. "Now, Charlie," he said, standing in the doorway. "When I stop by to ask you if you need anything, I don't mean a hamburger."

"I know, John," I said. "And I thank you for it."

"I'm asking if you need money," he continued. "I know you had to handle all the bills when Ira got shot, and I know you couldn't work."

He was right about that. And the worst part was that two or three months before, I'd had to borrow a thousand dollars from one of Betty's brothers in Memphis. And, of course, the rest of the family had informed him that he'd never see that thousand dollars again. I would have died and gone to hell with a broken back before I'd let them be right, but now it was time to pay up, and I didn't have the money.

"Tell you what," I said. "Now that it's out there, I really could use something."

"Is it money?" he asked.

"It is money," I said. "But it's serious money. Big money."

"All right," he said, "What do you call serious money?"

"A thousand dollars," I said.

He reached in his left front pocket, pulled out a stack of hundred dollar bills, counted out ten of them, and handed them to me. "Are you sure that's enough?" he asked.

"Yessir," I said. "Do you want me to draw up the IOU, or do you want to draw it up?"

He laughed and pushed the roll of bills back in his pocket. "There ain't gonna be no IOU, Charlie," he said.

"Well," I said. "Come the DJ convention later on in the fall, I'll have your money for you."

I meant it when I said it. And, sure enough, when the DJ convention came around, I'd caught up on the bills and saved up the money I owed him. And, just by coincidence, we were performing together on the same night. So I found him on the side stage, getting ready to go on, and I walked up to him with the thousand dollars in my right hand.

He turned and looked at the money. And then looked at me. "What's that?"

I poked it at him. "That's the thousand dollars I was supposed to pay you during the DJ convention," I said. "This here's the convention, and this here's your money."

He chuckled. "I'll tell you what, Charlie. I'll watch the trade papers, and when I see that you're worth at least a million dollars, I'll come and tell you that I need that thousand dollars. Now, get out of my face, I don't want to talk about this no more."

There was nothing I could do but hang my head and stick the money back in my pocket. So that's what I did.

He was that good of a friend, John was. We were two hillbillies, and any time a hillbilly trusts another hillbilly, there's gotta be more than just trust there. There's gotta be friendship. And John was the kind of person you were grateful your whole life to be friends with.

One of the saddest days of my life was when I went to the funeral for John's mother-in-law, Mother Maybelle Carter. Another was when I went to the funeral for John's mother. And then there was the funeral for John's wife, June. And when she left, the days were numbered for John. Everybody knew it, and everybody who knew him was sad all the time, waiting for the end.

June wasn't just John's lover, wife, and the mother of his children. She was also his nurse, caretaker, and dietician. He'd been sick for a long time, and she was the only one who had a handle on what he should and should not eat. On how to take care of him. When she passed, he didn't have any idea how to take care of himself. And I was at his funeral, too.

It's not very cool when you go to enough funerals to eradicate an entire family, an entire generation. It's the worst feeling in the world, if you want the truth. But I'll say this. I would fight with all I had for Johnny Cash's reputation. I know I don't need to now, but I would fight with everything I had for him. John was an extremely precious man, and there will never be another like him. He wasn't a taker, he was giver. And, sure, he had his faults, as we all do. But in the end, he conquered them all.

Johnny Cash and me

A few years after John died, his estate released an album called *Personal File*. It was an album he'd spent decades making. He'd just slip away from whatever he was doing and record one or two of the songs that meant the most to him, just him and his guitar. And one of the songs that he recorded was "When I Stop Dreaming," and he told the story of how he used to hide up in that pickup truck as a kid, so he could listen to Ira and I and Eddie Hill, playing together as the Lonesome Valley Trio. I couldn't stop crying when I heard that song.

It was a funny thing, but I talked to John hundreds of times there toward the end, and he never mentioned once that he'd recorded it. I guess that not knowing how long he would be around, he probably didn't want to mention it because it might never be released in my lifetime. But it was. And it meant the world to me.

CHAPTER 42

THE
BREAKUP

I'm still not sure why I stayed with Ira as long as I did after he started to go downhill with the drinking. I guess it was the only way I knew to make a living, and you don't just walk away from something that's been good to you. Maybe I was just nervous that I really couldn't do it without him. That's what he always told me, and it's hard not to believe something you get told over and over like that. But it was one bad show after another, most of them ending with him drunk, slurring, "When this trip's over, I'm quitting this fucking business. I've had enough of this shit. I've had enough of being told what to do, and I've had enough of you, Charlie."

It got to where I never knew if I was gonna be able to make a living from week to week. Finally, I couldn't take it anymore. I called up Ken Nelson and said, "Look, Ken, I don't know how much longer I'm going to be able to hold this together."

"Hold what together?" he said. "What are we talking about, Charlie?"

"The Louvin Brothers," I said. "The shows are a mess, almost every night. And he screws everything up. If I tell him there's important people watching and I need him sober just this once, he just tries that much harder to get drunk."

"Is it really that bad?" Ken asked.

"It's ruining my reputation, Ken," I said. "People never chalk it up to just Ira Louvin when a show goes wrong. It's always the Louvin Brothers. My name's in there, too."

"Do you want me to talk to him?" he asked.

"Everybody's tried to talk to him," I said. "There ain't no talking to him. What I want to know is if it does break up, can I still record for Capitol as a solo artist?"

"Waitaminute," he said. "If I say yes, it might make you do something hasty. And then if you can't make a living it'd be on my back."

"So that's a no?"

"No, it's not a no. It just means I won't answer this way. But if it does happen, then you call me."

"All right," I said, and hung up.

Well, it wasn't too long afterward that Ira and I played a date in Kansas City, and he really tied one on. He just got totally washed away in whiskey, and ended up with two or three women after the show. When I left him to go back to the hotel, he was leaning on the bar, a glass of booze in his hand, giving the ladies everything he had.

The next morning we had to leave early to get to Watseka, Illinois, for an afternoon show. I got up on time, showered and shaved, and went over to his bed and shook his shoulder. "Time to get moving, Ira," I said.

He didn't even stir.

I shook him again. "Come on, Ira. We got a drive ahead of us."

"I'll get up when I'm ready to get up," he mumbled.

"All right," I said. "But we got to get moving if we're gonna make the next show."

"Ah, go to hell, Charlie," he said. "We ain't never been late to a show. We've got plenty of time."

Of course that was bullshit, but I knew better than to argue with him. So I picked up my Val-A-Pak, my guitar, and his mandolin, and said, "I'll see you downstairs." And then I left. I figured that if nothing else, I could get the car loaded so it wouldn't need anything else but his Val-A-Pak with his clothes.

When I got outside it was cold and drizzling. Just a miserable morning. I set Ira's mandolin up against the building, where they had a pretty good bib to keep the rain off. Even though it was in a hard case, he always liked his mandolin on top of the Val-A-Paks, so I loaded my guitar and Jimmy Capps's guitar, and then our Val-A-Paks, and Jimmy and I stood out there waiting for him.

Finally, he came down and threw his Val-A-Pak in the van. Then he looked around. I could tell he had a monster of a hangover. The booze had really eaten him up by this time. His tall, hard good looks had melted away until he was just a skeleton of himself. "Where's my fucking mandolin?" he said.

"It's sitting right against the wall there," I said.

"Right there against the wall," he said. "Out in the rain."

"It ain't in the rain," I said. "They got a bib right there to keep the rain off."

"Who did it?" he said. "Who brought my mandolin out here and left it in the rain?"

"I already told you, it ain't in the rain."

"Who did it?"

"I did it," I said. "I was waiting until we got everything else loaded, because you like your mandolin on top of the Val-A-Paks."

"You don't ever touch my fucking mandolin again," he said.

"All right, Ira," I said. "Let's get loaded up."

"I mean it," he said. "Don't you ever touch my fucking mandolin again. Nobody touches it but me."

"Get in the car," I said. "We've got a long drive."

Well, he got in the car, finally, but the whole way from Kansas City to Watseka, he cussed me like a yard dog. And then when we got to the gig, which was an outside show, he found Ray Price, who was on the ticket with us. Ray was also a drinker, a bad one, and they got to really boozing it up on Ray's supply.

To give an idea of what he'd done to our reputation by that time, the date we were playing paid a total of twelve hundred and fifty dollars. And since Ray Price was the so-called star, he got a thousand of that, leaving us only two hundred and fifty dollars. And of that, we had to pay ten percent to the booker, and then thirty-five dollars a day for our picker. By the time we bought gas to get to and from Watseka, we didn't make as much as the musicians did.

As soon as we pulled out of the lot after the show, Ira started in on me again. "This is it," he said.

"It is?" I asked.

"Yeah," he said. "When we get home, I'm quitting this fucking business. I don't know what the hell you'll do without me, probably get yourself a job at a service station." He was always a real morale builder when he got drunk.

"You sure about that?" I said.

"I'm sure," he said. "I've had enough of this shit. I've had enough of being told what I can do and can't do. Of when I can stay and when I can go. I've had it with all of you."

"All right," I said. "If you're sure, then I'll tell you this. You're right."

"I know I'm right," he said.

"No," I said. "What I mean is that this is the last show we'll ever do together."

"That's what I said," he said.

"Right," I said. "But now I'm saying it, and I've never said it before. I want you to know that I'm not bullshitting you. We're gonna go home and that's it."

CHAPTER 43

ONSTAGE

I don't think he believed I would quit, but I was out of options. So when we got back, Betty and I took a vacation we had planned, picking my mother and father up in Alabama and driving them down to Florida. They'd never seen a lemon tree or an orange tree, and I wanted them to get the chance while they were still alive. We stayed down there a few days, and then rolled back on a Thursday. And when we got back, I called the Opry, told them Ira and I had split up, and asked if I could still come on solo for our show that Friday. And they said yes.

I've always lived well out of Nashville when I could, and back then, we were about sixty miles from town. That meant I had to get ready and rolling pretty early if I had a date on the Opry. So even though it was pretty early the next morning, I'd already taken a shower and was half shaved when the phone rang. "Hello," I answered.

"Hello, Charlie," Ira said. He sounded as jolly as could be. "What are you doing?"

"I'm getting ready to do the Opry," I said.

"Oh, you are?" he said. "What time are we on?"

"We're not on," I said.

He didn't talk for a few seconds. A long few seconds. Then he said, "What are you talking about, Charlie?"

"You know what I'm talking about," I said. "I'm on at eight, but we aren't. Not together."

"That doesn't make any sense, Charlie."

"Sure it does. You quit the other day and I agreed."

"Aw shit," he said, and he tried to laugh a little, "You know that was just that old liquor talking."

"Yeah," I said, "I know it was just the old liquor talking. But that's all I've heard for years, and I don't want to hear it no more. You and I ain't doing nothing together no more."

He got angry, all right. He started cussing pretty good, but I hung up on him. I imagine he probably busted a few of his instruments that morning, but it wasn't my problem anymore. As soon as I realized that, I couldn't stop grinning as I finished getting ready. Then I couldn't stop shaking from nerves. And it was then that I realized, too, that there was no Ira there to help me steady them.

I probably smoked two whole packs of cigarettes driving into Nashville. I felt like somebody had parked a truck on my chest. Of course, I'd been on that Opry stage alone before. There were times Ira didn't show up, and other times I wished he didn't. I was used to going ahead and doing what I had to do by myself. But I guess I expected the worst. Somebody to shout out, "Where's the other half?" or something like that.

Ira was always convinced that he was at least eighty percent of the act, and I was only the other piddlin' twenty percent. And he wasn't alone in thinking that. I know Chet

Back in a Nudie suit

Atkins and others have said the same. When Ira was living, everybody talked about his tenor and his songwriting. And I'm not denying that he was one of the greatest tenors and songwriters that every lived. I was very fortunate to be a part of that, to sing with him and get my musical learning that way. But I think I've proved that I was at least fifty percent of our act.

On every show we ever played, I did my part. I didn't get drunk, and I didn't throw tantrums. And he would show up so drunk he could barely stand, let alone sing. I don't know how many times that happened. Or his mandolin would get out of tune and he would sling it against the wall and then go back and stomp it. I thought hard about those times as I drove into Nashville.

Today, there's several hard rock groups that take their instruments, and beat one over the other, and bust them. Some even throw gas on them and set them on fire after they're finished. They destroy their instruments every night, and the companies that make the instruments just ship the next round to the next city, so that when the band gets to the next date they're already there. I guess the companies doing the donating feel that if they have a big rock group playing their instruments, then other smaller groups will want to play the same thing. So they just keep doing it.

It aches me to see people destroy an instrument onstage. Especially knowing that there's as many as a thousand teenagers setting out there that would give their eyeteeth to have them. Why not just walk out there and hand your guitar to some starry-eyed kid instead of smashing it? You'd make a lot more points with your fans than you would for the few people that enjoy watching you destroy it. But they don't do it that way. And Ira didn't, neither.

On the drive to Nashville, I thought about his tantrums onstage. And all of the times that he'd cut me down in front of people, too. Or would get drunk and disrespect our mother. And when I got onstage at the Opry, I was ready. I knew I was doing what I had to do.

Nobody yelled anything nasty at me onstage, either. I'd recorded one song solo called "Plenty of Everything But You," and that's what I played. A few of the people remembered it, or pretended to, and they applauded, which just about stopped my legs from quivering. I don't know if they were just being nice, but it didn't really matter. They made me feel at home, and that's all I needed. And when I was done, I went out and did two more shows on Saturday. Then I got a booker to book me solo, and the first thing you know, I was working more by myself than we ever had as a duet.

When a promoter hires an act and they screw them over, they ain't likely to get hired again. It doesn't matter how good they are. God knows, there's enough problems just promoting a show and getting it going without the band causing trouble. And that's what had happened. The news was out that if you wanted some real trouble with a show, hire the Louvin Brothers. But gradually I overcame that and proved myself to be dependable and sober.

CHAPTER 44

I
CAN'T FLY

Ira swore up and down that he was done with the business after we split up, so Papa gave him a couple acres, and Ira had a nice little home built on it for no down payment. We didn't see each other much after he moved back to Sand Mountain. I felt like a fly in the buttermilk whenever I visited, so I tried not to.

There were times we couldn't avoid dealing with each other, though. For one thing, I didn't want to just go by my own name, Charlie Louvin. I'd been a brother act all my life, and I wanted the name The Louvins. So I called Ira up and we came to an agreement. In exchange for me getting the name, I'd give up my half of two hundred of our best songs, leaving him as the sole writer. So we went to the Acuff-Rose publishing company together, and I had my name removed from the songs.

Ken Nelson wasn't buying it. I had a boy I'd picked out to sing high tenor and play lead guitar, but when I gave Ken the news, he just shook his head. "I don't give a shit what Ira said," he told me. "It won't be two months before he'll be wanting to record on his own."

"I don't think so," I said. "He says he's done with it."

"He'd be the first," Ken said. "But I'll tell you what, if you get a notarized letter from him releasing the name, you can use it."

"All right," I said. "Do me a favor and get your secretary to type one up that says what it's supposed to, and I'll get him to sign it."

Well, after I got the letter in the mail, I had it notarized, and then drove it down to Alabama. "Come in," Ira yelled when I banged on the door.

"Hello, Ira," I said. He was sitting alone on the couch, the curtains drawn, watching television and smoking a cigarette. As bad as he'd looked before we broke up, he looked worse now. When Ira and I were boys you'd still see people with consumption now and then, and that's what Ira looked like he had. Like his lungs had given up and he was just wasting away.

"What do you need, Charlie?" he said, without getting up.

I handed him the letter. "I have to get this signed so I can use the Louvin Brothers name."

He just looked at the paper for a minute. Then he read it, slowly, top to bottom. "You think I'm stupid?" he asked when he got done.

"No," I said. "I don't think you're stupid at all. This is what we agreed on verbally, it's just in writing. That's the only difference."

"I'm not signing that damn thing." He laughed at me. "Piss on you."

"Okay," I said. And there wasn't nothing to say after that, so I left.

I should have thanked him, though. It forced me to use

my own name, which I should have had the balls to do from the get-go. That's the way it is sometimes, I guess. You get forced to do what you should have done by yourself anyway. So I went ahead and recorded as Charlie Louvin.

Thank God for unanswered prayers. That's what I say. But it's been a long struggle. And I've never gotten used to not being a duet. Even today, surrounded by my band onstage, if I sing a Louvin Brothers song I'll scoot off to the left so Ira can come in when it comes time for the harmonies. I just cannot break that habit.

Ira did start recording, too. Just like Ken said he would. Ken gave me the news. I walked in to see him one day and he said, "I told you Ira'd be back within a month. He's wanting to record now."

I laughed at that. "Well, he ain't using the name The Louvins, that's for sure. We've been through that."

He had two single records, about three months apart. Neither one of 'em did shit. The first one was called, "Who Throwed That Rock?" It was a little novelty song. A guy was walking down the street with his girl, and a guy threw a rock at them and it missed her arm, but hit him in the ribs.

The other one was worse. He should have known better than to record it. It was a song Tommy Hill wrote, called "I Can't Fly." It was cursed if ever a song was. Jim Reeves recorded it and it wasn't two months until he was dead. And after that, there were as many as ten people who recorded it, and every one of them met an untimely death. I've had people try to get me to record that song, and I tell them, "You've gotta be crazy. This song's spooked." It's a good love song, but not worth dying over.

I tried to help Ira out whenever I could. At one point, he got pretty hard up for money, so I even set up one more Louvin Brothers show. There's this little town right up above where we were raised called Ider, and I got us a schoolhouse there. We advertised it real good, and we had a pretty darn good crowd. We sung together again just like the old days. It felt a little like one of our old Haynes family reunions. There's nothing like singing with your own blood, even when the circumstances aren't the best.

After the show was over, I got the money, and it was six or eight hundred dollars. "Hold out your hat, Ira," I said, and when he did, I poured all that cash in there for him. "That's what came in tonight," I said. "If you get hard up again, you can always call me. I'll be here."

He never said a word about why we broke up that night. Not one word about how it might've been a little bit his fault. Nothing like that.

After that show, I only saw him one more time. One night I walked off the Opry stage and Ernest Tubb and Ira were standing there together. Ernest was always kind of a fixer. If something was wrong, he would do whatever he could to help heal it. "Hey, Charlie," Ernest said, "why don't the both of you come on over and do a couple of numbers at the record shop show tonight?"

"I guess I could do that," I said. I couldn't really say no, after all.

"I don't know," Ira said, "I didn't bring my mandolin with me."

Well, Bill Monroe was standing about four feet away, and he pulled his mandolin off his shoulder, and handed it to Ira. "Here," he said. "You can use mine."

It took me about a full minute to get my mouth shut. I'd never known Bill Monroe to do that with anybody, anywhere. If you asked to see his mandolin, he'd hold it out for you to look at the front, and then flip it over and let you look at the back. "There," he'd say. "You've seen it." And then he'd put it away.

Of course, Ira couldn't say no after that, so we all walked

down to Ernest Tubb's record shop together. At that time, it was on Broadway, and Monroe went two or three doors down to Linebaugh's restaurant, where we met up with him after we played a couple songs. "Thank you, Bill," Ira said, handing his mandolin back to him.

"You're welcome, Ira," Bill said, putting the mandolin back in its case. "Sit down and have a cup of coffee with me. You, too, Charlie."

"She's quite an instrument," Ira said, taking a seat. "I mean it. Thank you."

"Anytime, Ira," Bill said.

"If there's ever anything I can do for you," Ira said, "You just let me know what it is."

"I'll tell you what," Bill said. "There is one thing you can do."

"What's that?" Ira said.

"When I die, you can sing a song at my funeral."

Late-night performance at the Ernest Tubb Record Shop

"What song?" Ira asked.

"Any song," Bill said. "You pick it."

Ira laughed. "All right, Bill," he said. "But just in case I don't make it to your funeral, I need you to make a promise."

"What's that?"

"I want you to sing 'Swing Low, Sweet Chariot' at mine."

That started Bill laughing, too. They sat there giggling over which one was gonna die first. I thought it was creepy as hell, but they were just giggling like a couple of girls.

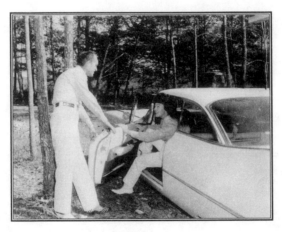

Ira and Anne

CHAPTER 45

THE
WRECK
ON THE
HIGHWAY

It was a Saturday night in June 1965. The band and I had played a show in Asheville, North Carolina. We'd been touring hard at the time, and we were just flat exhausted when we got offstage, so we all hopped in bed straight afterward to get some sleep before we had to start out for the next show in Virginia at Watermelon Park.

Well, I was still the one who got everybody up and moving, and I still did all the driving. So I woke everybody up at four o'clock the next morning, and more or less rolled the band from the bed to the car. And as we drove to the Virginia date, I never turned the radio on in the car. I guess I didn't want to wake up the guys. And then, when daylight came and the guys finally came awake of their own accord, we just left it off.

But when we finally got to the park, Sonny James, a country singer who was also on the ticket that day, was standing out front at the gate.

I pulled the car to a stop beside him and rolled down the window. "What's going on, Sonny?" I asked.

"You've got an emergency, Charlie," he said.

"An emergency?" I said. "What kind of emergency?"

"I don't know enough to say," he said. He handed me a slip of paper. "Back down the road there's a service station. Call that number."

I took one look at that number, and I spun the car around as fast as I could and roared for the service station. It was my number on that slip of paper, and it scared me to death. The only thing I could think was that Betty or one of my kids was hurt. "You and the kids all right?" I blurted out as soon as Betty picked up the phone.

"Me and the kids are fine," Betty said.

"Good," I said, breathing. "Good."

"It's not good," Betty said. "It's Ira."

"What do you mean it's Ira?" I said.

"They pulled me out of church this morning," she said. "There was a wreck in Kansas. Ira was killed, Charlie."

It'd happened in the middle of the night as it turned out, and if I had had the radio on at any point after about five o'clock in the morning, I'd have heard the news. Of course, maybe it was better that I didn't hear it. I probably wouldn't have done a very good job of driving if I had.

He'd played one of his solo shows in Kansas City. And instead of staying over in Kansas City, he'd decided to just come home. At exactly the halfway point between St. Louis and Kansas City is this place called Kingdom City. It's a big truck stop and a little village, a place you can stop and get a cup of coffee and a bite to eat.

That's exactly where the wreck happened. Ira's car ran straight into two guys who, according to Missouri law, were nine times over the legal limit for drunkenness. They were on their way from St. Louis to Kansas City to celebrate Father's Day, and they crossed over the yellow line and plowed straight into Ira's car. One witness estimated each car was doing about seventy-five miles per hour. When two cars hit at that speed, there ain't much chance for anybody.

It wasn't just Ira in the car, neither. His fourth wife, Anne, who I barely knew at all, was with him. She was a singer out of Canada that he'd married somewhere along the way. Also along for the ride were a couple friends of his, Billy and Adelle Barksdale, who lived around Sand Mountain. Billy was a manager at the Coca-Cola plant down there, and he played some electric guitar. He'd offered to play for Ira for nothing, and even did the driving in his brand new Chevrolet Bel Air. Ira, Billy, and Anne were killed outright. Adelle made it to the hospital, but she was dead on arrival.

Ira's car

I couldn't get a flight from Washington, DC, which was the nearest airport, until something like ten o'clock at night, so I went ahead and worked that date in Virginia. I had to do two shows. An afternoon and an evening show. They were the hardest shows I ever had to do. I couldn't do any Louvin Brothers songs, I knew I'd break down right there in front of everyone.

When I got done, one of the boys drove me to the Washington airport, and I arrived in Nashville later on. I don't remember the time, but my wife met me at the funeral home where the bodies were coming, bringing me everything she thought I'd need until the funeral was over.

CHAPTER 46

THE
FUNERAL

When Ira died, Bill Monroe was on a tour in the northeast that was set to continue for another two or three weeks. But he didn't finish that tour. He remembered what he'd promised to Ira, and he was there on the day of the funeral, singing "Swing Low, Sweet Chariot." He had the Jordanaires doing backup vocals, and I'd never heard him sing with a four-piece vocal group behind him, like a quartet. It was one of the best performances he ever gave.

I chose the preacher for the funeral. And I was careful to choose one who couldn't have told the truth about Ira if he'd wanted to. He only knew what I'd told him. Mama and Papa were there, of course. Papa held up real good, as I knew he would. But my mother had a softer heart than Papa did, and she was completely destroyed.

Betty and I paid for it all. Ira didn't even have a grave spot, so we gave him and his wife two places at the top of the mark we'd purchased. It was a new perpetual graveyard, and Ira and Anne were the first two people buried there.

Nobody thanked Betty and me, of course. In fact, Anne's mother and sister showed up at the funeral home to pick up the insurance check from the musician's union in Nashville, and they got in a fight over the money right there. They didn't ask, "Who bought this nice casket my sister or daughter is laid out in?" They just got the check and went back to California. That's about all I know about Anne. Ira was only married to her for little over a year, and I never did get to spend any time around her.

Papa and I never talked about Ira much after that. He was a very quiet man already, and he got quieter after the funeral. Mama and I talked, though. It turned out that just before leaving for that trip, Ira had told her that when he got back from Kansas City he was gonna use the money he made up there to buy a tent, and he was gonna start preaching, moving from place to place. "I've run away from God too long," he told her.

I never told Mama this, and I never would have for no amount of money, but a few days after Ira was killed, a Tennessee state trooper knocked on the door of my house in Hendersonville. "Yessir, what can I do for you?" I asked, answering the door.

"I've come to pick up Ira Louvin's driver's license," he said.

"Ira's driver's license?" I said. "What do you need that for?"

He kind of looked at me funny. "He didn't tell you?"

"Tell me what?"

"He was picked up for a DUI in Nashville a couple of weeks ago. He didn't appear for his court date, so I'm here to take his driver's license. Do you have him?"

"As a matter of fact, I do," I said. I turned around and walked back into the house, picked up a newspaper that had a picture of Ira on the front page, and held it up to him. "Here he is," I said. "You can rest assured he's in good hands, but if you need him, I'll do my best to get him for you."

"I'm sorry," the trooper said. And he left.

My gut feeling was that Ira stayed sober on the Kansas City trip, though. And I have friends who were there with him who say he was. I believe that God thought, "I might salvage something out of this yet, but I've gotta do it now." That's why I think he was killed. Because he'd promised that he was gonna be a different person when he got back. And the good Lord knew that he wasn't strong enough to do it.

CHAPTER 47

LAST DUET

It wasn't too long after Ira's death that I went to Kansas City to play a date. And driving down I-70, I remembered that I'd heard it said that the wreck was exactly a half mile east of Kingdom City. So I stopped along the side of the road and picked up some pieces of the cars. There was so much junk scattered around that it looked like both cars had been dynamited. That's what happens when two cars collide head-on like that, I guess.

The only thing that survived the wreck was Ira's Mandi-tar. It was an instrument that he'd designed himself, with the body of an electric mandolin, but only four keys and four strings instead of eight, so it wouldn't go out of tune as much. Which, knowing Ira, was a good thing. Toward the end, it was almost all he played, and it didn't have a scratch on it. I thought it deserved to be seen in the Country Music Hall of Fame, so that's where it's at now. I've always wondered at that, that the only thing that wasn't smashed to splinters was his own specially designed mandolin.

There's been a bunch of leaving songs throughout time. I always thought Reba McEntire sang the best one, which was titled simply "Somebody Should Leave." It's about a marriage that's gone wrong. Every time the husband and wife get together they just fight like dogs and cats, and they both know somebody has to leave, but neither of them can bear to do it.

In the case of Ira and me, it was me. I took on the blame. I was the culprit who walked away. But I don't think I had a choice. I just couldn't stay no longer. It was destroying the Louvin Brothers, and it was destroying me. I couldn't hold a family together not knowing how I was gonna make ends meet, or if he was even gonna stick around. The insecurity of not knowing is the worst kind of insecurity, and I couldn't take it anymore. You can't live like that, and you can't ask your family to, either.

I know it was better for Betty and the kids not having him around, too. Betty and him was just like a possum and a cat thrown over a clothesline with their tails tied together. They couldn't get along at all. He'd come to our house drunk at all hours, making an ass of himself, and she'd have to tell him to get out. "I don't want my kids to see you this way," she'd say. "Go home, go anywhere. Just get out of here." She was right, it wasn't fair to my children to have to see that. And it wasn't fair to her, either, to always be caught in the middle.

But even knowing all that, I couldn't stand there by the road holding the pieces of his car without thinking that he'd have still been alive if I hadn't left the duet. And it tore me apart. I won't pretend it didn't. I'm the biggest realist you'll ever meet. I think things happen in the order they were de-signed to happen. When it's really your time to go, you go, and it was his time. But even as true as that is, it didn't help very much as I stood there knowing that I'd never see him again. All the air went out of me and I got so choked up I thought I was gonna die. And then I just stood there and cried.

Then, one night the summer after Ira died, I was coming back down Highway 100 toward home. It was about ten o'clock at night, and I had to pass the graveyard where Ira was buried to get home. And, I don't really know why, but I got this powerful urge to see his grave. I hadn't been in a while, and I just wanted to sit with him for a minute or two.

So I pulled up in the graveyard, took my flashlight, and went up the walkway to his stone. When I got to it, I sat down on the bench. At this perpetual cemetery, they don't have raised tombstones, but they have metal benches that you can sit on, and I just sat there for a while, thinking about what might have been.

As I was sitting there, I heard a mandolin out of nowhere. It was just barely there, but it was sure enough a mandolin. And I realized it was the intro to a song I knew. A song that Ira and I had played together, one of the nineteenth-century songs we learned from our mother. And then I heard his voice singing the first verse. And when the harmonies came on after the first verse, I started singing along.

It wasn't just inside my head. I know the difference. It was out there in the world. We sung a whole chorus together, and when the next mandolin turnaround started, it got weaker and weaker, until finally it disappeared. But we sung a verse and a chorus of that old tragic song together before it was gone.

And I knew from singing that song with him that he was where he was supposed to be. And that he understood that I hadn't had no choice but to do what I did.

After the song was over, I sat there for three or four more minutes without moving, hoping that he'd kick off another one. But it didn't happen. And I suppose I knew it wouldn't. I'd spent my whole life singing with him, all the way back to when we learned "Mary of the Wild Moor" from our mother, and I was just grateful that I'd gotten the chance to say good-bye to him in this, the only way that mattered. The harmonies we sang, they were still in my blood, and they couldn't be taken away.

So I got up and walked away, back to my car. Knowing that we'd sing together again. Just not here.

CHAPTER 48

REUNION

It wasn't three years after Ira died that Smilin' Eddie Hill, our first manager, picked up this hellish headache that would not go away. It plagued him so long that he finally went to the Vanderbilt hospital in Nashville. They examined him and just couldn't find no reason for him to have it, so the doctor told him, "I think you're just overworked, Eddie. Take a couple of weeks off."

Well, Eddie took his advice, and left Memphis with his wife to go to Hawaii. But when he got out there, the headache got so bad he couldn't stand it, so he returned to Vanderbilt. They stripped him down and put him on the table where they did x-rays. But before they could get the x-ray machine going, he had a stroke.

The doctors said Eddie would remain a vegetable his whole life. He didn't quite, but he couldn't walk without two men holding on to him, and he had to take little, bitty steps.

If you turned him loose, his feet would keep going, and he'd fall backward just like a big old tree.

His wife had to work. Had to, just to have some eating money. Before she left for work every morning, she'd lay him back on the bed, and when she got home that night, he would be in that exact same position. After all his tomcattin' around, she never had to wonder where he was ever again.

I really felt sorry for him. So a couple years after the stroke, I stopped by his house to talk to his wife, Jackie. My band and I were going to Stumptown, which was where Eddie was born, and I wanted to ask her if there was any way we could take him with us.

"Yeah," she said. "You're welcome to take him with you. But you better have a couple of good men with you. He's a devil."

The tour bus

"I have a drummer that's as big as he is," I said. "We can handle him."

Well, we got started to Stumptown, and she was right, he was a devil. He wouldn't let us bring him anything when we stopped. Not food, not a soda, nothing. He just had to go out and get it for himself, which meant me and the drummer pretty much had to carry him. He did it the whole way there.

He couldn't keep track of what he was saying, either. At the time, I had this big tour bus, and it was something else. I mean, it made Roy Acuff's air-cooled Franklin that had impressed Ira and I so much look like a Volkswagen Beetle. And every few minutes Eddie would sit up, look around, and say, "Boy, Charlie, if me, you, and old Ira'd had something like this, we'd have been tough, wouldn't we?"

"We sure would have, Eddie," I'd say. Over and over again.

When we pulled up in Stumptown, there was a bunch of rough-looking old boys there waiting for us. They had a pickup truck with a wheelchair in the back of it, and four of them picked Eddie up, planted his ass in that wheelchair, and tied him into it. Then they took him everywhere. All over town, telling him all about the stuff they'd done together. It was something to see, they way they took care of him.

When the show got going, he was backstage acting like he was having so much fun that I told the audience, "I'll tell you what we're gonna do fans. We're gonna get Smilin' Eddie Hill up here to do his favorite song, 'Milk Cow Blues.'" And those good old boys pushed him up front, and set him up in front by the microphone, and he sung the shit out of that song. Didn't miss a word.

CHAPTER 49

BACK HOME

A couple years later, Betty and I went down to Papa's house and did something we should have done long before. While he was gone for the day, we brought an electrician and a plumber in to build a bathroom in a corner of the back bedroom. Then we got a couple good, strong men to carry the cook stove out on the back porch and had the kitchen wired for a stove and a water heater.

Of course, Papa pitched a fucking fit when he saw that stove sitting on the front porch. "What in the hell happened here? Who's the idiot who moved my stove out on the porch?"

I was waiting for him, and I put my hand on his shoulder. "Come on in, Papa," I said. "Let's take a look."

He looked around at where the woodstove used to be, and then said, "Well, what're we gonna do about heat during the wintertime, now?"

I laughed. "Get you a heater, you cheap devil."

It took him a while, but he finally got used to some of those nice things. But he never would take a crap in the commode. "You don't do that in the house," he'd say, and he'd walk out a third of the mile across the road when he needed to.

Papa never owned a good vehicle until fourteen years later, when I finally got him a brand spanking new Chevy truck. I'd asked him time and time again to let me buy him a vehicle and he'd always said no. So finally, I got tired of asking, and I just bought it. That still makes me want to kick my own butt, thinking about how many times I could have put him in a decent set of wheels before that.

I remember how when people started driving automobiles to church it always seemed that Papa was a little embarrassed about his transportation. His old pickup truck was about used up. If he drove it one day, he'd have to pull it upside of the house that night, raise his hood, get his spark plug wrench, and take all six of his spark plugs out. Then he'd bring them inside, put them in the fireplace to burn the oil out of them, and then blow and brush them out before he'd install them back in the truck. That was the only way he could keep it running. But still, we never missed a day of church. He made sure of that.

That was Papa's way. He did what he had to do. And as hard as he was on us kids, and especially Ira, I think he always did the best he could with what he had. Which, if you think about it, was true of Ira as well. Just as it's true of all of us.

Six months after I bought him that new truck, Papa had a stroke and died. My mother lived for two years after him. Papa probably would have lived that long, but he had high blood pressure, and hid it from everybody. If he got to feeling too rotten, he'd swipe one of Mama's blood pressure pills, but he wouldn't go to the doctor. If I had known it,

I'd have hog-tied and took him whether or not he wanted to go.

But it wouldn't have mattered. We leave when our time's up. I have to believe that. And I suppose there's no use in feeling too bad about how little help he'd take from me.

CHAPTER 50

SOLO

One of the last things I ever imagined would happen without Ira is that I'd be back on the country charts as much as I was. But I ended up with thirty singles on the charts. Most as a solo artist, but a few as a duet after I teamed up with Melba Montgomery. We got two top ten hits out of that, "Something to Brag About" and "Did You Ever." I even got four Grammy nominations, the last one when I was eighty years old.

One day, while I was in the studio, I met a guy there who was sweeping the floors and cleaning the ashtrays. He was a Rhodes Scholar, a helicopter pilot, and a Captain in the Army, but he was working as a janitor, if you can believe it. Well, I was looking to record a couple songs, and he come passing by me, and he whispered in my ear on the way, "I believe I've got a song you'd like."

"All right," I said, "let's hear it."

He shook his head. "I can't play it for you here, they'll fire me. That's one of the rules. I'm not allowed to plug songs."

"You got it on cassette tape?"

"Yes."

"And you have the words?"

"Yes."

"Well," I said, "You go ahead and lay 'em on that little old desk over there when you get a minute."

Well, I went ahead and recorded the first song, and sure enough, when I looked over on the desk, there lay a cassette tape and a copy of the lyrics. And when the A&R man that was running the session said, "Okay, guys, what's the next song?" I went over and picked up the tape, and read off, "I'm Always on the Outside Looking In." Then I gave it to the session leader, he put it in the machine, and while they played the tune so that the band could learn it, I learned it, too, with-

With Kris Kristofferson

out letting on that's what I was doing. It was the second song on the session.

The janitor was just beside himself that anybody could learn a song that quick. Still, he knew it was one thing to get a song recorded, but another to get it released. So he was even more excited when they went ahead and released it.

From then on, that janitor and I were friends, and we still are. His name was Kris Kristofferson, and he ended up making a whole lot more money with his songs and acting than I ever did. Along with giving Johnny Cash that seat to our show, recording that song of Kristofferson's, and helping him get his start is one of the things I'm proudest of.

The truth is I had help from as many people as I've helped. More, actually. Alison Krauss has been right there to help

Alison Krauss and me

me when I needed it most. Willie Nelson's helped me out, too. He showed up in the studio one day with his gopher carrying his old guitar and amp, and we ended up doing a song with Waylon Jennings called "Makin' Music." There's a lyric in the chorus about how we all hope somebody remembers our name when it's all said and done, and at the end, Waylon jumped in and said, "We'll always remember your name, Charlie." That meant a lot to me, that a singer as good as Waylon would say something like that. And there have been lots of other people, too, who've been there for me when I thought my career was all but finished. People who I barely knew, who owed me nothing, who helped me.

One guy I probably owe as much to as anybody is Gram Parsons. Unfortunately, I never got to meet him, but he was a Louvin Brothers nut. When Ira and I were playing with Elvis on that one tour we did, we stopped in Waycross, Georgia, and Gram, who was only nine years old at the time, was in

Getting some help

the audience. He went on to work with three or four rock and roll groups, and every time he'd con 'em into playing a Louvin Brothers song or two. Whether it was a gospel song like "The Christian Life" or a secular song like "Cash on the Barrelhead," he'd get them to record something. He was responsible for introducing the Louvin Brothers music to a great number of people. His first recruit was Emmylou Harris, and I can't say how much she's helped me over the years.

And it wasn't just country singers. The last time I did a show in Vegas, Ray Charles was playing on the strip, and a friend of mine worked it out so that I could go and watch him perform. Ray Charles has always been one of my favorite performers. Well, right in the middle of the show, Ray finished a song and said, "I'm gonna sing one of my favorite

Inducted into the Country Music Hall of Fame, 2001

songs right now, and from what I hear, one of the writers is in the audience." Well, just when he said that, the spotlight reached out across the audience and landed on me. "I'd appreciate if he would just stand up." I could scarcely believe it, but I did stand, and Ray continued, "Ladies and gentlemen, Mr. Charlie Louvin." Then he thanked me, and he and all his girls sang, "When I Stop Dreaming."

It turned out he knew I was in town and had pretty much arranged the whole thing. I didn't even know that he knew who I was, let along that he was a fan of some of our songs. I was so excited I could barely stand it.

People ask constantly, "When you and Ira were recording those songs did you ever think they'd still be this vibrant sixty years later?" Well, anybody would be a damn fool to say, "Oh, yeah, we knew that." So, I tell the truth, that I didn't know nothing of the sort. We were merely trying to make a living, that's all we were trying to do.

Makin' music with Willie

EPILOGUE

I spend a lot of time thinking about old age now. I guess everybody who gets old does. Lately, I've been thinking that maybe Ira's lucky he didn't make it.

Old age is different from anything you'll ever encounter in your life. Your head will lie to you, your heart will lie to you, and your pecker will lie to you. You'll see something sitting there that you used to handle with one hand, just pick it up and sling it, and your head will tell you, "Are you kidding, man? You've lifted twice that much." Then you'll grab ahold of it and find out that it's more than you can handle. Those golden years they talk about, they're bullshit. I knew Ira awful well, and I don't think he could have handled it.

The only thing that doesn't bother me about getting old is dying. I'm not scared of it, not even a little bit. I sure as hell ain't been a saint, but I don't owe any of my friends an apology for anything I've said or thought, either. My conscience can go up or down, but I don't have to worry about feeling pain for something I did to someone else. I don't hate and I don't hold onto grudges. There are people who do, but I ain't one of them.

One thing I'm proud of is that I had more hits as a solo artist than Ira and I ever did as the Louvin Brothers. It always did get under my skin how folks would say that Ira was the only one of us who had any talent.

I had a good run with Capitol Records as a solo artist. But

it ended in 1972, when Ken Nelson got transferred to the West Coast and was no longer the A&R man for Nashville. I got another deal with United Artists, but I only put out one album with them. The change in country music was beginning to take effect, and my days were numbered. Chet Atkins always used to say that he carried country music uptown, and he did. But in the same sentence, he'd continue, "And maybe we carried it too far."

Beginning in the 1980s, most country artists were crossover artists. It was a complete top-to-bottom turnover in the kind of music you hear on country radio stations, and we still haven't recovered. Country music ain't country music now. The so-called country artists now get it as close to pop and rock as they can and still call it country. I got tired of playing their game, so I didn't record anything, except for one tribute album to Jim and Jesse McReynolds, for two decades.

The Opry hasn't fared any better. The longer you've been at the Opry, the worse they treat you. That's the truth of it. They treat you ten times worse than they treat the people who come onstage with one song out. But they're the boss and it's their Opry, and they'll tell you in a New York minute, "If you don't like it, go somewhere where they run a show you like." They'd be happy if every one of us old-timers dropped dead tomorrow. But I'm gonna be just like a bad tooth. I'm gonna hang in there so's I can annoy as many of them as I can.

I know how they work. I ought to. I've had more years with the Opry than anyone. They give that honor to Jimmy Dickens, but it ain't his. See, when they fired Jim Denny, that stage manager we auditioned for so many times, he took a bunch of artists with him, and Jimmy Dickens was one of them. And that meant that Jimmy Dickens was gone from the Opry from 1956 to 1968, about twelve years. So he's not the longest-running member of the Grand Ole Opry. I am. He's six years behind me.

Me with the Grand Ole Opry cast

But life goes on. And I guess if you wanna keep living you have to face the world as it is. You can't change the things you really want to, anyway. You can try, but once something's done, it's history. And common sense will tell you that you can't change history.

I shouldn't complain. I've enjoyed my solo career immensely. And lately, I've been happy to start recording again. In 2000, I was sitting in my living room one morning, and my telephone rang from New York. It was a guy named Josh Rosenthal, and he informed me that he was a big Louvin Brothers fan. It turned out he owned a record company, Tompkins Square, and asked if I would be interested in cutting a record. He said he had distribution, and that's what most private labels don't have, so we put out a record and he promoted the hell out of it. We did well together. We put out two studio albums, two live albums, and a gospel album.

There are times when I wish we could have stayed together, Ira and me. But the drinking made it unlivable. At the beginning of my solo career, I'd get hung up when people'd come to a show and request a Louvin Brothers song. Back when we first broke up, it would kindly annoy me. Hell, it'd come close to pissing me off. But now I try to remember the good things about the Louvin Brothers. Especially before the Opry, when we were just starting out with Smilin' Eddie Hill, and it felt like we could do anything we set out to do. So I just play the songs.

I've had my trials and tribulations, but I've been doing my extreme best to enjoy the life I have now. Even if I'm just sitting on my porch in the sunshine and smoking a cigarette, I believe I'm as happy as God can make any man. Happy, appreciative, and thankful. I can envy some of 'em, the ones that drive the Hummers and Rolls-Royces, even the air-cooled Franklins, but I have everything I need or want.

Well, except maybe a Harley. I'd like to have a small Harley, where I could put both feet on the ground and stop at a light. I don't want one where you have to let it lean and hold it up with one foot. I don't want one of them at all, but I'd like to have a small Harley.

If Betty weren't so afraid of motorcycles, I'd buy one. But she's probably right. I'd probably go out and get my neck broke.

*Charlie Louvin passed away on January 26, 2011,
of complications from pancreatic cancer, two months
after this book was completed. He was 83. His final
thoughts were an expression of gratitude for the life
he lived and the people he got to live it with.*

Charlie and Ira's graves

ACKNOWLEDGMENTS

Benjamin Whitmer would like to thank his wife, Brooky, and his children, Maddie and Jack, for putting up with his absences, and presences, during this project. He'd also like to thank Neil Strauss, Anthony Bozza, and Monique Sacks of Igniter Books, whose generosity and guidance could not have been more appreciated. And, of course, his agent, Gary Heidt, for sticking with him.

PHOTO CREDITS

p. 44   Hine
p. 112   Gordon Gillingham photograph © Grand Ole Opry
p. 142   Les Leverette
p. 182   Gordon Gillingham photograph © Grand Ole Opry
p. 191   Courtesy of Capitol Records, LLC
p. 210   © Grand Ole Opry
p. 228   Courtesy of Capitol Records, LLC
p. 263   Sid O'Berry photograph © Grand Ole Opry

All other photographs courtesy of
the family of Charlie Louvin

SELECTED LYRICS

KNOXVILLE GIRL

I met a little girl in Knoxville
A town we all know well
And every Sunday evening
Out in her home I'd dwell

We went to take an evening walk
About a mile from town
I picked a stick up off the ground
And knocked that fair girl down

She fell down on her bended knees
For mercy she did cry
Oh, Willy dear, don't kill me here
I'm unprepared to die

She never spoke another word
I only beat her more
Until the ground around me
Within her blood did flow

I took her by her golden curls
And I drug her 'round and 'round
Throwing her into the river
That flows through Knoxville town

Go down, go down, you Knoxville girl
With the dark and roving eyes
Go down, go down, you Knoxville girl
You can never be my bride

I started back to Knoxville
Got there about midnight
My mother she was worried
And woke up in a fright

Saying, "Dear son, what have you done
To bloody your clothes so?"
I told my anxious mother
I was bleeding at my nose

I called for me a candle
To light myself to bed
I called for me a handkerchief
To bind my aching head

Rolled and tumbled the whole night through
As troubles was for me
Like flames of hell around my bed
And in my eyes could see

They carried me down to Knoxville
And put me in a cell
My friends all tried to get me out
But none could go my bail

I'm here to waste my life away down
In this dirty old jail
Because I murdered that Knoxville girl
The girl I loved so well

THE KNEELING DRUNKARD'S PLEA

"Lord have mercy on me"
Was the kneeling drunkard's plea
And as he knelt there on the ground
I know that God from heaven looked down

I went down by an old country church
I saw a drunkard stagger and lurch
And as he reached his mother's grave
I saw that drunkard kneel and pray

"Lord have mercy on me"
Was the kneeling drunkard's plea
And as he knelt there on the ground
I know that God from heaven looked down

"Bring my darling boy to me"
Was his mother's dying plea
And as he staggered through the gate
Alas, he came just one day too late

Three years have passed since she went away
Her son is sleeping beside her today
And I know that in heaven, his mother he'll see
For God has heard that drunkard's plea

"Lord have mercy on me"
Was the kneeling drunkard's plea
And as he knelt there on the ground
I know that God from heaven looked down

GREAT ATOMIC POWER

Do you fear this man's invention
That they call atomic power
Are we all in great confusion
Do we know the time or hour

When a terrible explosion
May rain down upon our land
Leaving horrible destruction
Blotting out the works of man

Are you, are you ready
For that great atomic power
Will you rise and meet your savior in the air

Will you shout or will you cry
When the fire rains from on high
Are you ready for that great atomic power

There is one way to escape
And be prepared to meet the Lord
Give your heart and soul to Jesus
He will be your shielding sword

He will surely stand beside you
And you'll never taste of death
For your soul will fly to safety
And eternal peace and rest

Are you, are you ready
For that great atomic power
Will you rise and meet your savior in the air

Will you shout or will you cry
When the fire rains from on high
Are you ready for that great atomic power

There's an army who can conquer
All the enemy's great band
It's the regiment of Christians
Guided by the Savior's hand

When the mushroom of destruction
Falls in all its fury great
God will surely save His children
From that awful awful fate

Are you, are you ready
For that great atomic power
Will you rise and meet your savior in the air

Will you shout or will you cry
When the fire rains from on high
Are you ready for that great atomic power

IRA

You were the king of Sand Mountain
At least I thought so
You had a knack for high tenor
And I sang the low
Alabama to the Opry
Was the second hardest road
The worst was me losing you
And singing all alone

Ira, I still hear you
Off in the distance
Your sweet harmony
Ira, I still miss you
There'll never be another
'Cause you can't beat family
I know you're up there singing
With the angels, Hallelujah, Ira

Mandolin strings still ringing
In my memory
There were times when you gave Bill Monroe
A run for his money
You had a way with writing
Music from the heart
Your voice is strong
Even though you're gone
'Cause I still hear your part

Ira, I still hear you
Off in the distance
Your sweet harmony
Ira, I still miss you
There'll never be another
'Cause you can't beat family
I know you're up there singing
With the angels, Hallelujah, Ira

One day soon I'll sing with you
And the angels, Hallelujah, Ira